# TEACHING YEAR ONE

Edited by Lucy Hall

Published by Scholastic Ltd.
Villiers House
Clarendon Avenue
Leamington Spa
Warwickshire CV32 5PR

2 3 4 5 6 7 8 9 0          8 9 0 1 2 3 4 5 6 7

## Authors

Paul Noble, George Hunt, Peter Clarke, Terry Jennings, Margaret Mackintosh,
Dorothy Tipton, Gillian Robinson, Pauline Boorman, Richard Ager, Lynn Newton,
Doug Newton, Geoffrey Teece

## Series Editor

Lucy Hall

## Editors

Irene Goodacre, Clare Miller

## Series Designer

Lynne Joesbury

## Designer

Mark Udall

## Illustrations

Maggie Downer

## Cover photograph

Fiona Pragoff

Designed using Adobe Pagemaker

British Library Cataloguing-in-Publication Data
A catalogue record for this book is available from the British Library

ISBN 0 590 53819 5

# Contents

4 **Preface**

5 **Your Class** Paul Noble

15 **Curriculum and Classroom Planning** Paul Noble

21 **English** George Hunt

43 **Mathematics** Peter Clarke

67 **Science** Terry Jennings

85 **History** Paul Noble

95 **Geography** Margaret Mackintosh

105 **Music** Dorothy Tipton

117 **Art** Gillian Robinson

127 **Physical Education** Pauline Boorman

139 **Information Technology** Richard Ager

143 **Design and Technology** Lynn Newton and Douglas Newton

153 **Religious Education** Geoffrey Teece

# Preface

Primary school teachers don't say, as secondary teachers would, 'I teach history'. They say 'I teach year 4s' or 'I teach a reception class'. Why, then, have all the books for primary teachers been wholly subject-orientated? Primary teachers have had to buy about 13 different books and read through them all to extract the relevant bits.

It was about 20 years ago, that the thought occurred to me that it would make teachers' lives much easier if all the information about teaching their year group was provided in *one* book. Since then I have been waiting for someone to do it. But no one did. So, finally, fourteen different authors, Scholastic and I have put together the seven *Primary Teacher Yearbooks*.

I should like to thank all the authors. They faced a difficult task in tailoring their writing to a common format and structuring their guidance, about what to teach and what to expect from children, so that it correlated with the seven different stages of the primary school. They have all been extremely patient.

Particular thanks are due to Paul Noble, who not only wrote 13 chapters in the series, but was also deeply involved in the development of the project from the very beginning. His practical, knowledgeable advice and cheerful imperturbability kept the whole project stuck together.

We all hope that you will find your Yearbook useful and that it meets your needs – whichever class you teach.

Lucy Hall, Series Editor

# Your Class

As the National Curriculum applies to children of compulsory school age only, (children in, and after, the term after that in which their fifth birthday falls), Year 1 is children's first complete National Curriculum class in the school.

Teaching emphasis is now on core national curriculum subjects and the equipment and organisation that goes with them, although there will continue to be a reducing need for activities such as water and sand play. As work becomes more structured, so the arrangement of the classroom needs to be a little different from that of a reception class.

## Planning your classroom

Ideally every child should have his or her own space and storage drawer, desk or shelf and there should be enough furniture for all the children in the class to be seated simultaneously at desks. However, the need for an area where all the children can collect together for 'carpet' time and any other specific teaching that demands collective concentration on the teacher is paramount. It may therefore make sense to start the organisation of your classroom by identifying where that space is going to be.

If you are teaching Year 1 for the first time, or if you have moved to an unfamiliar room, it is worth carrying out a stock check. This is best done by listing equipment according to subjects and further sub-dividing into useful categories such as furniture, games, expendables and tools. It is easy to persuade yourself that this tedious task is unnecessary, but if you do it you will be set up for the rest of the year and will avoid the nasty surprise of finding out, after you have got the equipment out, that you haven't got room for it!

Decide what you are going to display and what you are going to store, and where. You may wish to keep the broad divisions of the classroom commonly used in reception rooms (wet area, dry area, book corner and so on) or go for finer demarcations. Some teachers simply decide on how many areas they want and then label them by colour. This has the benefit of allowing the function of each area to be changed without changing the name by which the children know it - they will know where the green area is even if it is the maths area one week and the writing area another!

The argument for having tables grouped in blocks to provide large working spaces and opportunities for talk are at their strongest throughout Key Stage 1, and it is unusual to find other arrangements such as rows. However you decide to do this, think first about your children and what you want the seating arrangement to do for them, as well as for you.

## Starting the new year

Be ready for your class on the first day of the term – which means, be early. Have a very clear strategy for dealing with parents who wish to engage you in a long dialogue in the morning. Children have a priority call upon your time and you need to make this clear. The ground rules for admitting children to the classroom and dealing with parents may well have been established in reception, but if they have not, then be quite clear and firm about the rules you are going to apply.

Generally it is better if children are greeted at the door and separated from parents there. Year 1 children should no longer need a parent to hang up their coat or carry their lunch box, although your judgement about this will depend upon the space available and the nature of the children in your class.

Domestic arrangements and the ground rules under which your class will operate come next. If common practices are used throughout the school then the children should not get too confused when they move from class to class, nevertheless each teacher operates in slightly different ways. Remember children may have forgotten the routines that they knew before the long summer break, so you must allow plenty of time for these to become re-established.

## Learning names

On the first morning (and possibly every morning if you wish) collect the children together on the carpet and begin the day from there. A 'name game' is a good way to start as it gives you a chance to mark the register and, at the same time, start to identify each child by name (if you are not already familiar with the class). You might, for example, give out pre-prepared labels for each child to wear (one for yourself) or make them as the first exercise of the day.

One useful strategy is to have prepared bold name cards, (about 30 cm in length) on one side of which is a photograph of the child. (Your school's computerised record system may contain a suitable portrait.) Laminate the cards, or cover them in self-adhesive plastic film, and fix a string handle to each one. Use these frequently, particularly in the first few weeks, to label a place, a piece of work, a display, or even the child.

'Me and my toys' is a memory game variation on a familiar theme. One child says, for example: *I am Charlotte Lennon and I have a purple bike.* The next child makes his statement and repeats the previous one: *I am Peter Robinson and I have a toy monkey. She is Charlotte Lennon and she has a purple bike.* Carry this on around the class as far as you can go.

You might also try a guess-the-child game. *I see someone with big brown eyes and short curly hair wearing black shoes with the laces undone! Who is it?* The children can join in by setting the questions.

## Information they should have

Although you will need to establish classroom rules quite quickly, don't overwhelm the children with too many pieces of information at once – you should get them involved in practical work as soon as possible – but put their minds at rest on specific matters that might worry them.

Here is a list for you to consider:

- Where are the toilets? What do I do if I want to go to the toilet during lessons/playtimes/lunchtimes?
- Where can we play at playtime? What do I do if I have a problem at playtime?
- What are the 'First Aid' procedures that we need to know?
- Where do we eat our lunch?
- Which entrances are we allowed to use? Which areas are 'out-of-bounds'?
- What do I do with my lunch box? When can we fetch our lunch boxes?
- Where do I sit? Which is my drawer?
- Where do I put my PE kit? Is my name on any clothes I take off?
- How do I get my teacher's attention?
- Are there any rules for moving around the classroom?
- Who can touch the computers, and when?
- Where are the tissues if I have a runny nose? Can I take one whenever I want?

- What bells and alarms will we hear? What about fire drill and emergency exits?
- What are the rules about bringing toys to school?
- Can I eat sweets or snacks? If so, what and when?
- What are the rules about litter?
- Tidying up? Who does what, and when?
- What should I keep in my drawer? Can I bring pencils to school?
- What are the rules about using rubbers and scissors?
- Teacher's desk - what rules apply?
- Running and walking in school - what are the rules?
- What should I do with dinner money, letters for teacher and so on?

Some children may be new to the school or to your part of the building so it is important to make sure that everyone understands the geography of the place. Children can be in school for quite a while before they have cause to find out where 'the office' is. It is often best to assume ignorance.

*Who is the headteacher? Secretary? Caretaker? Where would you find them?*

# Social and emotional development

Most difficult of all to establish are moral codes and standards of behaviour. Establishing that, for example, 'in this school we care for each other,' is a process that never ends. Nevertheless, rules like these need to be spelled out and attention should be drawn to them whenever an opportunity arises. Broad principles like these are important because they underpin numerous detailed edicts about bullying, racism, fighting and so on. There are no short cuts. Establish them in the children's minds by telling and repeating them, by demonstration, by example, and by enforcement, and start straight away. Most Year 1 children have already begun to appreciate the rules that govern how we all behave so this is a good year in which to consolidate them.

## Behaviour issues

Bad behaviour, especially that which disrupts the class, is generally made up of a pattern of small incidents, rather than a single extreme outbreak. These small irritations may ultimately prove the most intractable so record them (the constant furtive jabbing of another child with a pencil; repeated manifestations of the inability to share anything; masturbation; inappropriate language, and so on).

Managing a child's behaviour at the age of 5 or 6 is no different from at any other age. You need to have clear standards, be consistent in their application, use praise and rewards to reinforce good conduct, and enforce a range of sanctions to discourage inappropriate or undesirable actions. Children's behaviour, especially if it is extreme or out of character, will be an indication of stress. In Year 1 they will be as sensitive as at any time in their school career to death, birth, marital conflicts, moving home and so on. In Year 1, however, they are much more likely to speak openly about these things, which is good for the child, but not so easy for the teacher, who must be ready to deal with this situation. 'My grandpa died today and I'm sad,' is the sort of statement that may suddenly be thrown at you when you are marking the register, but it is even more difficult when a child talks of a fight at home or other private domestic affairs in front of the class. Young children are, of course, easily distracted and you may have to side-step issues when the situation or circumstances are difficult, but a child with problems of this sort on his mind is not likely to be able to apply himself to schoolwork. You need to give him time and reassurance. Most often a truly distressed child will need holding and the comfort of human contact.

# What can I expect of Year 1 children?

Moving from reception to Year 1 does not suddenly transform children into totally different creatures, but at this time change is taking place at a fairly rapid rate. Vocabulary is expanding markedly and differences between individuals start becoming clearer. Some Year 1 children will still be quite babyish and you will notice a widening of the behaviour and performance gap between mature, intelligent children and the rest. Although it is just as risky to generalise about children as it is to generalise about adults, a few general comments about Year 1 pupils may be useful.

It is particularly important to remember that you are dealing with children who are still very young. (Sometimes it is easy to forget this, especially with children who are big for their age.) They first make sense of the world through very simple distinctions and their use of language is a guide to this. Year 1 children are more likely to operate in the world of happy or sad than in the world of elated or miserable.

Children at this age cannot yet function completely independently, but there is less need for them to be 'handfed' than before. Parents (or teachers) should be required less often to assist in tasks such as taking off coats or shoes. They are perfectly able to do these things for themselves, and this independence needs to be encouraged. (Some mums may need instruction on this point.)

As the children are now much more capable of independent action, you will now be able to operate systems in the classroom that require children to take on a little responsibility. If pens and paper are made accessible, the children can be instructed to fetch what they need. Monitors can be employed for the first time and children can be trusted to take on the tasks of giving out trays of coloured pencils, collecting work, or returning the register to the office.

They are now able to memorise simple routines (indeed they will be quick to remind you if you forget them) and can be taught to do start-of-the-day tasks and end-of-the-day clearing-up. This is actually a critical time in the training of children  to be tidy, to be considerate of others and so on. For, although they are still self-centred, they are beginning to be aware of the needs of others around them.

## Relationships

Children, at this time, are also beginning to be aware of their own strengths and weaknesses, and this shows in their behaviour. It is during Year 1 and Year 2 that certain groups and individuals may become over-physical as they test out the boundaries of their own and others' strength. They can also be very vocal about the behaviour of others: *She pinched me!; John stole my rubber!* One of the reasons for this is that these young children are unable to see the broader picture and rarely see the other person's point of view. It may even be necessary to explain to them when an issue has been resolved: *Are they quiet now?; Is Cara behaving properly now?*

This inability to see the broader picture may cause Year 1 children to become involved in a lot of petty-minded bickering. You need to give them time to think for themselves as they gradually learn to see another's point of view: *Adam kicked me...but it was an accident!*

They will happily play with other children of whatever gender and it is not unusual for little boys to invite little girls to their parties and vice versa. By and large they still play together 'separately' but they are beginning to formulate notions of what it is to have a friend. Indignant and sometimes distressed children will come to you declaring that: *Lisa says she won't be my friend!* or that *Gary says I can't play with him.* All they are doing here is testing out their new-found power of words. This is normal, but can be upsetting (often to parents as much as to the children themselves). Truly isolated children, however, pose an entirely different problem. They are generally easy to spot because they will seek their own space and appear to be unaffected by whether others play with them or not.

## Toilets

By Year 1, children are a little more able to control their visits to the toilet, so periods of class instruction or story are less likely to be interrupted. Introduce and enforce a rule about not getting up to leave on these occasions and operate a simple peg system for toilet visits at other times. (You place a peg against your name when you visit the toilet – the number of pegs is limited and therefore the number in the toilets at any one time is controlled.)

Schools do not always have urinals and boys of this age are usually too impatient (or desperate) to wait for their turn to use the toilet so they will share – resulting in inevitable spillage. One effective solution to this problem is to place a target (sticky-back plastic) on the bowl or urinal. It works like magic.

## Concentration span

Although the children's levels of control and concentration may have increased, they will still only be able to concentrate for short periods of time and you need to plan your work with plenty of changes and variety. In some European countries teachers use a song or a game to punctuate lessons every 15 minutes or so!

# Children with special needs

If you have done your homework with the pupil records you will be aware of any children in the class who, because of the nature of their special need, have already been picked up by the system. These children may, before long, transfer to special units or other provision.

Generally, in Year 1, judgements can be formed about those children within the normal range of need (Stage 1 to Stage 4 of the Code of Practice) in order to place them on the Special Needs register, often for the first time. Take a little time over this and beware of making hasty judgements about SEN designation in the first few weeks.

It is critically important that you involve parents from the start and that the Code of Practice is explained to them. This tends to be a particular responsibility at Year 1 because it is often the first time that parents become aware that their child has special educational needs. Your SENCO may well take responsibility for the initial discussion. On average, one in five of your class will be on the register. You will need to arrange an early meeting with your SENCO to discuss extra provision or the involvement of outside agencies.

Mostly special needs will have to be met by you in the classroom. This means putting aside time to plan how you are going to differentiate work for these children. Be disciplined about this or you may find that SEN occupies all your time. You might consider setting aside one evening a week to focus on special needs. Most of your SEN children will need reception-type provision in order to function at their appropriate level. You will also need to differentiate by your allocation of time. They will need more adult attention either from you or your classroom support assistant.

Casual help from parents is invaluable throughout Key Stage 1 but particularly when you require adults who can listen to and talk with the less able. Language development is, of course, critical to success in other subjects so use as much parental help as you can get. This resource also needs to be managed effectively, so spend time planning exactly what you want your parent helpers to do. A good idea is to have a training session for parents, instructing them in basic listening, speaking and reading-response skills.

# Mobile children

There may be special groups within the class (travellers; or children of parents in the services or on overseas placement) who require particular help. At bottom their needs are the same as any other child in the class and you should not lose sight of this fact. Do not treat them as if they are odd and be careful not to respond to stereotypical images. Dealing with a non-English-speaking child of a Japanese businessman in Britain for six months does pose practical problems somewhat different from those presented by the child of an RAF sergeant who has moved three times in a year, but they both need reassurance, attention, and appropriate work to help them feel happy and secure.

# ESL children

Non-English-speaking children can pose the biggest problem initially simply because English is the main medium of instruction. Ironically, this is usually almost completely overcome within about 18 months. Ultimately these bilingual children can be an asset to the school so don't panic when you first encounter them. Schools dealing with large numbers usually have special provision and expertise that enables them to cope (language assistants perhaps) but if non-English-speakers are a new problem to the school you should find that the LEA will be able to offer practical advice and help. Children who start reception as non-English-speakers will, by Year 1, already have acquired enough functional English to operate quite happily with their English-speaking peers.

# Health and disability problems

Where special needs are physical, rather than educational, you need to do a certain amount of homework. Make sure you know what to do if a child has a fit or needs medication for asthma. You are not expected to be a doctor or nurse but for your own peace of mind make sure you know what to do in an emergency. Check that there are no problems with the arrangement or furnishing of your classroom that might pose a problem for any disabled child in your class. Report any problems to your headteacher.

Asthma is now such a common complaint that the management of inhalers and other medication can become a problem. Medicines should never be stored casually in the classroom and some schools choose to operate a central storage and administration procedure. Ideally several (if not all) members of staff will have received instruction in dealing with asthma and the regular use of inhalers should be properly organised. The onus is on you to be adequately informed.

# Log of incidents and behaviour

It is a good idea to keep a log of incidents and behaviour that might ultimately require action. This will provide useful evidence for other agencies and substantiate actions that you might need to take. Both health incidents (time and place of fits for example) and behaviour problems are worth recording.

Particular needs are, by definition, particular, and it is not possible to give advice for every eventuality. However exceptional a child's needs may seem to you, there will be established patterns of good practice which you can follow. Seek advice. Your head can contact outside agencies if necessary. Where physical disability is involved, the parents are likely to have made themselves experts in their child's needs, so be sure to consult them.

# Home-school issues

Good home-school relationships are critical to success in dealing with a whole range of issues - special educational needs, behaviour and medical problems. As always, the main object of working with parents is to get them on your side. Quite simply, the child's education has a better chance of success if parents and teacher work as a team, so this is in everyone's interests, especially the child's. Regular contact is the best guarantee of success otherwise minor problems have time to develop into major ones.

For example, if a child has a persistent bad smell because of poor bladder control or lack of hygiene, then this must be dealt with through the parents rather than the child. It is best to act straight away (by phone, if possible) and get the parents to take remedial action. Treat the issue as commonplace but as something that, for the comfort of everybody, including the child, cannot be ignored.

Share successes as well as problems with parents. The very act of bringing matters out into the open can be healing, but tread warily. Nobody likes being 'told off' and your words of dissatisfaction or complaint will live on long after your words of praise have faded.

Removing the professional barriers that once kept parents at arm's length does bring with it new problems and responsibilities. You must not allow parents to come between you and your ability to do the job. The lingering gossip first thing in the morning is the most common example. Parents will confide in you, and may even shock you with the frankness of their confidences, but it makes sense to stop them when you think that they are telling you something that you don't need to know. Redirect the conversation towards your concern for the child or refer them to the headteacher. Sometimes an individual can have a real

problem that they simply must share with someone (such as violence in the home).

# Health education

Dealing with health education issues, particularly sex education and substance abuse as well as moral issues and making distinctions between right and wrong, can only be done in a fairly straightforward, black and white way. *This is good for you, that is not. This is right, that is wrong.* Children of this age are happy to accept this level of direction, however, in order to make this approach work you need to be honest, and to explain matters directly and logically.

The first rule is never to teach a child something that will have to be unlearned at a later stage. Because an explanation is simple, it does not mean that it must be false. Reproduction can, and should, be dealt with accurately at the level of the children's comprehension and within the bounds of their need to know.

The second rule, that you should provide a logical explanation, is clearly linked to the first. Drugs education for a Year 1 child begins with discussion of things that we put into our bodies that are good for us and things that we put into our bodies that are bad for us. Some foods make us grow into healthy people, some make us sick. It is easy to build from there.

# Stranger danger

'Stranger danger' is now more of an issue that it was in previous years. As the children become more independent and have greater freedom, their need to understand some of the dangers in the world grows. Again, simple distinctions apply. Some people are good and some are bad (with emphasis on the good) but how can we tell? Fortunately, there is more help and expertise available to help you to do this effectively than ever before and the local police can usually provide material helpful in getting across a balanced message.

# Curriculum and Classroom Planning

Year 1 children are the first to be taught the full National Curriculum for the subjects of English, mathematics, science and information technology (the focus for national assessments), plus a balanced curriculum drawn from design and technology, history, geography, art, music and physical education.

Additionally, Year 1 children must receive religious education. This is not nationally prescribed but is set by a locally administered Standing Advisory Committee on Religious Education (SACRE). Most schools will work to some form of Agreed Syllabus for RE.

## Making plans

Curriculum planning is predominantly about delivering content which boils down to *long-term*, *medium-term* and *short-term* plans. It doesn't matter which year group you are teaching, the planning framework is the same. Be brief, selective and, above all, be realistic.

Long-term is the broad outline of work across the whole year. This will be planned well in advance (usually in the preceding summer term) and should be easy and relatively enjoyable. Easy, because it should be largely a matter of transferring material from the school's schemes of work; enjoyable because you will be able to make some choices about the type of projects, visits and programmes that you will undertake in the coming year. Regard it as a creative process. Do long-term planning early and do not waste time on detail.

Medium-term plans, which deal with the term's work or, more commonly, with the half-term's work, require more detail. A typical half-term plan would be a grid showing subjects along the top against 7/8 numbered weeks down the side. With experience, it is possible to set realistic targets for a week's work in each subject, but it is still a good idea to include a slack period to allow time for 'catching up'. The most common error is to plan too much work.

Short-term plans cover the day-to-day management of your teaching in the classroom. *What am I going to do today? What broadcast am I watching? What work is to be done by the special needs children and when? What is the classroom support assistant going to do? Are there any visitors, festivals or other disruptions to the routine.*

Short-term plans are notepad-and-pencil plans and fit alongside your timetable which sets the time framework for everything that you do. (Don't forget to note down your playground duty week and so on.) Some school managements regard these short-term plans as private documents, other heads will want a copy on their desk by the end of Friday. OFSTED inspectors like to know that this kind of daily planning goes on but do not always ask for evidence.

# Subject plans

Expectations vary from school to school, but you may also be expected to produce detailed subject plans showing content, concepts and skills to be taught, activities, resources, visits, and outcomes. You may even be required to produce a written evaluation of the project once work has been completed. Although such working plans are useful, the burden of producing them or every subject and every project is clearly time-consuming and may take effort away from teaching, preparing and marking. It is in your pupils' interests, as well as your own, that you keep control of this process and sort out priorities. Know when to stop.

There are ways to alleviate the problem of planning. Some schools pool their teaching plans and use them again and again when content is revisited. Others simply make the production of plans a joint effort and set aside time to do them (possibly on teacher-training days). Often, detailed project plans are produced by subject co-ordinators as part of the school's schemes of work so that if, for example, the school has decided to do a project on India, the plan is available for use. Plans are also available in commercially-published schemes. These may not fit your requirements exactly, but they offer a good way of cutting corners.

# Balance

Balance is perhaps one of the most difficult things to achieve in your curriculum planning. You will have to build in the Literacy Hour and the Numeracy Hour. You must also attempt to balance the requirements of the various subjects. The best advice is to think of balance over the longer, rather than the shorter term. Balancing history, against IT, against DT, against music, and so on, becomes a nonsense if you attempt to do it on a weekly basis. Look at a term's work and try to get some sort of balance there. In Year 1, literacy, numeracy and work related to these skills should dominate your teaching.

# Allocating time

Although time allocations are still a matter for the teacher to decide and there is no legal framework laid down (with the Literacy and Numeracy Hours this could be said to be changing) guidelines have been produced by QCA suggesting allocation of time by subjects.

Children in Year 1 like routine – they like to know where they are and what they are supposed to be doing, so consider communicating part of your daily planning to them. You might, for example, have a Day Board on which activities for the day are shown. This kind of device can be refined and used in a more active way. Some teachers, having decided upon the groupings for the day's activities use a dial with a moving hand which points to the activity or area that the class or groups should be engaged in at a given time.

You will definitely need 'odd time' activities set out for the children to use as the concentration span of a child in Year 1 is very short. Activities such as sorting boxes, busy books, a 'make' table and a 'tinkering' table are all useful, as well as specific number, reading and writing tables with 'odd time' work on them.

# Getting Organised

## Progression

In Year 1 you must make sure that you move your children on from the point they reached at the end of their reception year – so you must plan for progression. Your classroom may not look significantly different from the reception class but you must make sure that it is not a mirror image.

Progression is the key. A reduction in the use of sand and water play areas should be matched by the introduction of more demanding construction toys. In Year 1 the emphasis should move from 'playing with' to 'making'.

Similarly, the computer programs that you use and the books that you display in the library area, should become more challenging. The children should be fed new and more demanding fare. Selection of resources is one way in which progression can be planned for.

## Resources

Put out your basic resources in the places where you will most often need them. Have a central point for brushes, wax crayons and so on. Each table or group may well have its own small island of resources and a collecting box for finished and unfinished work. Typically, each child might be provided with a writing book or journal, a maths book, a writing line guide, a look-cover-write check book and a number line printed on card. Reading books, plastic homework bags, and 'try' spelling books may also be kept centrally.

You know the topics and subjects that you are going to be covering in the course of the year, you also know when each one will be encountered. Decide on the resource materials that you can provide in-house. Your school's subject co-ordinators will probably have produced resource lists as part of the school's schemes of work. Use these lists.

Next, decide what you expect the children to provide. Some topics on colour or materials can be almost fully resourced from home.

With these things decided, you will be ready to look to museums and other outside resource centres to plug any gaps that you find. You will need plenty of reading books because thin books are quickly read! Try to exercise control over the quality of books as well as the quantity. (Don't put too many out at once.) Make sure you have high quality books in the reading corner and change these regularly. Use the library service.

Have a Book Hospital so that children know what to do when they come across a book that is damaged. Try to teach respect for books and always keep a few special 'oo – ah!' books (usually the fragile, expensive ones) for sharing with the children as a treat.

Non-fiction must be catered for as well as story and you may choose to have a 'Find Out About' shelf or corner. Remember that it is possible to have too many resources and that Year 1 children can gain a great deal from very little. If you overwhelm them with objects they will be as confused as you are when you receive too much advice on how to teach!

## Audio-visual aids

Similar advice must be given about audio visual aids in the classroom. Use as many as you can cope with, and no more. You may be limited by the number of sockets available, especially if your classroom is an old one. Nowadays most Year 1 classrooms have one or two computers, although by the time you read this, this number may have increased. Keep the software you are going to use to hand and put the rest away. The effective use of a few programs is better than the confusion of excess. Have some method of recording computer and other audio-visual use – perhaps a tick chart by the side of the relevant machine.

As the year progresses, you should be able to trust your more confident children to teach others how to do basic operations on the computer (put the disk in; use shift and break;

follow simple instructions on the screen) and you should not need to be so heavily involved.

You must decide for yourself which additional equipment you will employ but, in Year 1, you can start to make use of tape recorders coupled with a distribution box and headphones, as well as more specialist equipment such as the Language Master. Most electrical equipment can be used more competently as the children get older – although the equipment itself may actually be most useful when the children are very young. If you do not have an adult to work with the children on such equipment, then don't use it.

## Clearing up

Being organised for Year 1s is not solely about what you do before school starts, it is also about the mundane, but potentially fraught, process of clearing up. Tidying up is a very real part of the children's education and is about becoming responsible people. Allow plenty of time for it to happen. Warn the children when the clearing-up period is about to happen so they do not start any new activities.

Stop before you start is a good principle. Settle the class before you allocate tasks and make sure that all the children know where to go (carpet or desk) when they have finished. You might like to use a clock to time the period or devise some other form of target or incentive. Tell the children precisely what you expect them to do. *Put all the brushes in the box please, Danielle* – not – *Perhaps you might like to collect the brushes, Danielle?* Precise use of language is not only critical to making things happen the way that you want them to, but also helps the child's own thinking and language development.

## People

Apart from organising your classroom assistant, you should think carefully about how to use your voluntary help. You can be more formal with employed staff and should have regular sit-down consultations with them. Casual parent help can be more problematic.

Don't have more people in the classroom than you can cope with and make sure that someone finds time to communicate the basic do's and don'ts of the classroom. Many teachers run into trouble because they do not limit the help they are offered. Three mornings for exampleis quite a lot to cope with but you must make your own judgement.

## Visits and visitors

You should aim to get your Year 1 class out and about as often as possible. The value of a visit diminishes with the distance travelled. An advance visit by you is virtually essential, and every visit must be tightly focused. Make sure that you do not trundle your six year olds around the entire British Museum or travel sixty miles to an arboretum when there is a perfectly good park ten minutes' walk.

The scope for entertaining outside visitors increases in Year 1 as curriculum content becomes more precise. Mums and dads are an underused resource, although the more sophisticated their occupation the less use the person often is. Most Year 1 children will not fully understand what their parents do for a living and a parental visit can be most rewarding. Be wary of occupations that may cause contention. Use your judgement!

A local policeman or policewoman might be invited to talk about stranger danger, or the school nurse to talk about hygiene. Year 1 children are more able to cope with this sort of advice than reception children, but make sure that you prepare the ground and that you

know your children and your visitor. Year 1 children are still capable of being scared out of their wits very easily and you do not wish to be the cause of nightmares. Plan the questions the children are going to ask and what they are going to tell the visitor.

# Specific subject preparation

In Year 1 you will not only start to teach subjects but will start to use the words associated with them. Be aware that the children will not naturally know what 'geography' is, only introduce words like these when the time is right and even then only with explanation.

But, even in Year 1, subjects can make specific demands of you. Geography requires familiarity with maps; in RE you will need to introduce holy books and religious buildings; history might demand some form of timeline; IT involves computers (obviously); and for art you will need a 'wet' area, somewhere to wash brushes and to dry pictures.

The subject sections in this book will offer you advice on what you should have in your classroom for each subject but it is up to you to take the overview. Don't have too many things competing for the children's attention, such as large displays for every subject. As Year 1 children will not naturally draw subject boundaries, your displays may well group together materials  under thematic headings rather than subjects. This is normal infant practice and neither the National Curriculum nor OFSTED requires that you change it.

## Display

Ask yourself, *Do the children need this display?* If the answer is 'No' then don't do it. Everything that you do plan to show should be displayed properly. Double-mount whenever possible, always get things straight and use a little imagination. Ask for advice from a colleague or read a book on the subject if you are unsure, you cannot afford to be less than competent – people will judge your class by its wrapping.

Two small tips: always crop or trim work on a Rotatrim, especially artwork, even if you don't think that it needs it; and if you work to an outside border then the interior of a display will usually take care of itself.

You will need to display a number line; the alphabet; number bonds; and selected letter blends. You will also need to display the materials you want the children to have access to. A space must be set aside for the stacking of children's workbooks and papers. You may not be able to have a music-making table available at all times but it is a good thing if you can.

Keep health and safety issues in mind at all times. Store heavy objects low down (you should have steps in your classroom or nearby so that you are not tempted to balance on tables to reach onto high shelves!). Liquids must be stored so that spillage is unlikely and you should take the obvious precautions in relation to scissors and adhesive.

# The teaching

This book is essentially a practical guide, but research has offered some pointers as to what makes a class teacher effective and efficient. For example, when activities are set up for young children, they often understand *what* they are to do but not *why* they are doing it. Here are a few suggestions for making your teaching efficient:

Don't do non-essential or menial tasks that could be done by the children or an ancillary.

Share your learning intentions with the children. (If a visitor asks a child what she is doing, will the answer be a learning objective?).

- Make sure the children have a clear understanding of what they are to do before they are sent off to do it (this may seem obvious, but it is still very important!).
- Tell the class what *you* are going to do during the activity.
- Step-by-step instructions are best and remind the children from time to time what they should be doing.
- Make sure they know what to do when the task is complete (have other tasks ready).
- Ensure that the physical arrangement of the class will help you to be efficient.
- Make the necessary resources accessible to the children.
- Arrange the furniture to allow for an easy flow of movement.
- Ensure that groupings are appropriate to the tasks.
- A 'good' lesson has a beginning, a middle, and an end. If you think about what you are going to do in each of these three phases then you are on your way to success. Make sure that the phases are clearly defined.

## Homework

Homework is still virtually a dirty word in many infant schools and yet the KS1 teacher has probably always been the most consistent provider of homework in any of the primary classes. Reading, and the pressure to succeed in this basic skill, has been the main reason.

Your school will probably have agreed a policy about homework. Some parents may play one teacher off against another if they detect inconsistencies . Parents of Year 1 children are very keen about such things as reading books! When you send materials home (and other material as well) make sure that they can stand the 'drink-dribble-baby-sister' test. Plastic zip-up folders are one solution.

## Reading records

Keep duplicate reading records because, if you rely on book marker cards, these will inevitably be dropped and lost. Your private records can document not only dates, Levels, pages and books but notes on test scores, knowledge of letter sounds, blends and digraphs and so on.

Use 'Home-School' books or something similar. A small standard exercise book will do. Parents should not only see what is written in the book but should add to it. You will learn much from these comments and you should encourage parents (and classroom helpers who might also use the system) to be honest but positive, purposeful and tactful.

As well as reading books, children in Year 1 may take home books, sheets or cards to learn letter sounds, and as the year progresses a few spellings to practise. Work taken home will affect children's progress, especially in reading skills, but you will need to educate parents in supporting and encouraging their children rather than pressuring them.

## At the end of the day

Homework is no good unless it reaches home so make the 'homework bag check' part of your end-of-day routine. Most Year 1 classes will gather together for a story or a song at the end of the day. Then comes the vital final check. With Year 1 children it is still necessary to ask: *Have you got your bag? Have you got your book? Have you got your jumper?* And when the child answers 'Yes', the experienced teacher will often then ask: *Where is it?* Too often it will then be discovered that – yes, he does have it – in his drawer! In this oft-repeated scene is encapsulated what Year 1 teaching is all about.

# English
## including Literacy Hour

The National Curriculum requires that competence in English should be developed within an integrated programme of speaking and listening, reading and writing, reflecting the fact that these four modes of language use can reinforce and support each other. The thoughts and experiences that children talk about can be related to the stories that they read and hear; these stories should encourage them to discuss ideas; the ideas can then form the basis of the children's own writing; this written work can be read and discussed by others; and so on in a continual creative spiral.

This is, of course, an ideal picture, and much easier to describe than to establish. In Year 1, however, it is important to set this spiral in motion by giving children lots of opportunities to talk about their interests and concerns and to listen reflectively to other people doing the same. They should also be encouraged to tell and retell stories, join in with poems and songs which contain rhythmic patterns, and participate in simple drama activities.

The National Literary Strategy specifies that children of this age should be introduced to a range of literature, including both stories and poems close to their own experiences, those from a range of cultures and others which are based in folklore and fantasy. The children should become familiar with, the features and uses of a variety of non-fiction, including material presented in electronic formats.

For writing, you will need to organise activities which demonstrate: 'the value of writing as a means of remembering, communicating, organising and developing ideas and information, and as a source of enjoyment.'

The most effective way to expose children to such a range of experiences is to enable children to contribute to the practical and recreational uses of writing in the classroom. Include them in practical task where reading and writing skills can be used. Helping to draft letters to parents, writing labels and captions for displays, and seeing their oral stories word processed, published and read out, are all useful experiences which will help to fulfil this general objective.

## Literacy Hour

The teaching framework devised by the National Literacy Strategy *Framework for Teaching* was the foundation for the Literacy Hour which was introduced into primary schools in September 1998. This one hour every day of dedicated teaching of reading and writing involves a rhythmic transition from whole-class teaching to small-group work and back again.

During this hour, children are engaged in work at whole text level involving comprehension and composition, work at sentence level involving grammar and punctuation, and work at word level involving vocabulary and spelling.

Suggestions for the type of work that might be done at each level in Year 1 are outlined in the Practical Ideas section on page 32.

# Key skills

Development and support of children's use and enjoyment of fiction, non-fiction and poetry should be integrated with the teaching of the key skills that children will need if they are to become independent readers and writers. These include:

- knowing the alphabet and how its printed symbols relate to sounds in spoken language;
- recognising how consistent letter patterns may reflect aspects of word meaning (unhappy, unusual, unkind);
- acquiring a sight vocabulary of instantly-recognised high frequency words;
- knowing how to use the grammatical structure of sentences and the overall meaning of reading material to help identify unfamiliar words;
- using knowledge of the alphabet and common letter strings to spell words;
- planning, drafting and reviewing written work;
- beginning to understand and use punctuation;
- forming handwritten letters legibly and fluently.

# What should they be able to do?

## Key areas: Speaking

Most children in Year 1 will have had at least one term in school, during which they will have been exposed to a variety of new experiences, and a vastly expanded range of people (both adults and children) to talk and listen to. These experiences will have helped to nurture the spontaneous talkativeness shown by many children at this age, although by the start of Year 1 this may have been tempered by some of the constraints imposed by the rituals of school life. Year 1 children will already be used to listening for their names in the register, keeping silent (or almost so) during assembly and story time, and talking more quietly when they are working in class than when they are out in the playground. These adjustments should not, however, be taken for granted, nor should they be regarded as an unmixed blessing. The differences between how language is used at home and how it is used at school can continue to be a source of confusion and frustration for some Year 1 children, and a conformity to the constraints mentioned above can disguise inhibitions arising from these tensions.

With a little encouragement, most Year 1 children are able to talk vividly and eloquently. They can recall and describe their own experiences in great detail, retell stories that they have heard read aloud and speculate about what might happen next, and offer ideas to explain why things are as they are. When they have nobody else to talk to, they will talk to themselves, experimenting with real or nonsense words, reciting rhymes or jingles, even talking their way through problems or imaginary adventures as they work and play.

Listening to these children talking, you might at first think that there is little difference between their speaking skills and those of adults. Indeed, many of the major features of adult speech will already be in place by the age of six, when most children are able to pronounce, accurately or approximately, all the 44 or so phonemes of spoken English. Some may still be learning to wrap their tongues around more complex consonant clusters (like *str-* at the beginning of words and *-mps* at the end) and to make the finer distinctions between similar sounds such as *f* and *th*. (In some dialects, of course, the *f* is substituted for *th* by all age-groups.)

Most children start school with a productive vocabulary (the words that they can actually say) well in excess of three thousand words. By the time they start Year 1 it can be assumed that maturation, combined with school experiences, social interaction and, perhaps, the development of literacy, will have added dramatically to this total. They will have learned new words about largely school-based pursuits like mathematics, science and PE. Their broadening social world will provide them with lots of opportunities to share new enthusiasms and associated vocabulary with other children, as well as to learn some fresh colloquialisms. Also, and very significantly, the school's concern with speaking and listening, reading and writing, will have enabled them to start building up a bank of words with which to talk and think about language itself. For example, in the field of literacy, words like *word*, *letter* and *sound* will have been presented to them with extended and potentially confusing meanings.

They will still have a lot to learn about the semantics, or meaning patterns, of the words that they are using – they may not fully *grasp* the different uses of closely-related pairs of words such as *tell* and *ask* or *big* and *long*. They may also find it difficult to understand the relationships between more general terms (like *animal*) and the particular terms (such as *horse* or *lion*) which come under these.

Children of this age have limited understanding of the fact that the same word can mean different things according to the conversation in which it occurs, and that the same object can be called different things depending on the perspective from which it is being viewed. This can often lead to confusion. You need to use language consistently, while making it clear, when appropriate, that different words can mean the same thing. Asking a novice reader a question like 'What sound does that letter make?', makes very little sense when the teacher or helper is pointing to a seemingly noiseless printed mark in a book.

The answer to such communication difficulties is not the rote learning of the meanings of ambiguous or specialised terms, but rich exposure to such words in natural conversations between adult and child. As long as the adult is aware of potential confusion, then it should be possible to devise situations in which the meanings of terms are demonstrated.

# Organising their words

By the age of six most children have amassed an impressive amount of expertise in grammar, in the sense that they know intuitively how to combine words to produce utterances that other people around them will understand. (This is not referring to the ability to speak standard English dialect or to understand formal grammatical terminology.) Six-year-olds are able to organise words into coherent sentences, and sentences into longer stretches of discourse, using rules similar to those which adults use to organise their speech. The example of speech below, from Kerry (aged six) talking about a visitor to her school, might help to illustrate this.

*The van came into the playground and the policeman showed us the dungeon inside and we saw bars for the robbers and a grille for the dogs and there was boxes and chains and things. We sitted in the driver's seat and he said if we was naughty he'd have to take us away but if we was good he'd show us the van. He had a tie that falled off so nobody could strangle him and he had two belts on, one for all his truncheon and radio and handcuffs and stuff, and one to keep his trousers up.*

There are several features of this extract that identify it as the speech of a young child, most noticeably the repetitive use of the connective 'and' to join fairly short and simple clauses. Even so, the underlying pattern of structures is similar to that which would be used by a mature speaker of the language. This straightforward, informative and humorous account contains an interesting variety of clause structures:

- subject + verb + object (*We saw bars for the robbers and a grille for the dogs)*;
- subject + verb + adverbial (*The van came into the playground*);
- subject + verb + indirect object + direct object (*The policemen showed us the dungeon inside*).

There is also an example of complex subordination:

*He said*

  (that) *if we was naughty*

    (then) *he'd have to take us away*

and this structure is co-ordinated with one of similar complexity

  (*but if we was good he'd show us the van.*)

Such complexity in speech is an important and impressive achievement. There is no need for a teacher to over-emphasise the relatively minor ways in which the child's language differs from that of an adult. Too much importance should not be given to on minor 'errors' (such as the use of *we was* rather than *we were*) as these might be features of the child's dialect, or (like *all his truncheon*) the result of using fairly rapid, informal speech while reporting an exciting event.

In any case, drawing undue attention to this in the course of a classroom conversation would simply impede easy communication. If the account were later written out, however, it would be appropriate to point out one of the features of subject/verb agreement in standard English.

The use of *sitted* as the past tense of *sit* rather than the irregular *sat*, and the similar use of *falled* rather than *fell* is a very common feature of children's speech at this age. Younger children often use the correct form to begin with, then unlearn this when they discover the rule that *-ed* indicates the past tense. The irregular form is usually relearned at about this age or slightly later, a process hinted at by Kerry's correct use of *came* as the past tense of *come*. This process of relearning does not require any specific teaching.

Six-year-olds use a limited number of linking words and phrases when they are speaking. The frequent use of *and* (as noted in Kerry's account) often gives a somewhat repetitive texture to children's speech. Though this is not the only linking word that they use, they will not develop the great diversity of words and phrases that give adult speech its characteristic rhythms (*of course, on the other hand, luckily, eventually*, and so on) until much later. There are exceptions, of course. Young children frequently take a liking to particular words or turns of phrase. They can often surprise their listeners by preceding remarks with such mature-sounding phrases as *actually*, or *as a matter of fact*, or ending them with items like *I expect* or even *Would you believe it?*

When it comes to the kind of 'public' speaking required by school activities such as discussion and recitation, children of this age will still have a lot to learn about the needs of audiences larger and less familiar than family and friends. However, by the end of the year, given sufficient supportive experience, they should be beginning to adapt their speech and their listening behaviour accordingly.

## Key area: Listening

You need to teach the children to listen sympathetically and thoughtfully, especially if they have had no nursery experience and only a term in reception. Help them to decide on sensible rules for good listening. Listeners, obviously, should be quiet and considerate, but point out that there are also benefits in comparing what is being said to their own experience, and in thinking of appropriate questions.

If you encourage this type of active listening from the start, and give children opportunities to voice their responses afterwards, by the end of the year most of the class will probably have become accustomed to it. (Provided, of course, that what they have been listening to has been interesting and relevant.)

# Key area: Reading

The majority of children in any Year 1 class will bring with them, from home and from the reception class, some fundamental skills and concepts about reading and writing, and will be capable of engaging in these activities at different levels of competence.

All of the children will have heard stories and poems and will have joined in with songs and rhymes. They will have personal favourites from this oral repertoire which they may have memorised to different degrees. This stockpile of shared experience is an important foundation for much early work in reading, so in the early days of the autumn term it is important to talk to the class, individually, and as a group, to find out what these favourites are.

Activities in reception will have given pupils some idea of the uses to which reading can be put. Children who have enjoyed reading will have favourite books and stories that they will turn to with the same feeling of reassurance that they might derive from a familiar toy. They may have 'made friends' with characters from reading schemes or series books, and will be keen to share their further adventures. They will look forward to taking new books home from school, and either reading them to their families, or listening to them being read aloud.

Most children will be aware of the range of uses that printed words are put to. They will have seen adults at home consulting newspapers, recipes, product labels and television listings. They will know that many books in their school contain explanations and information about real events – they may be capable of using simple reference books to answer their own questions. They will have seen their reception class teacher using written language to keep them, and other people, informed about various classroom rules and routines. They may also have helped to create and deploy writing of this kind.

By the end of Year 1, every child in the class should have participated in the production and use of a range of such documents.

Through shared activities such as the reading aloud of 'Big Books' with a group, or watching competent readers point to words as they read aloud, many of the children will have obtained a firm grasp of the one-to-one match between spoken and written words. They should then have an understanding that writing represents language in a consistent way, so that the same book always tells the same story, the same caption always delivers the same message.

| Word | | |
|---|---|---|
| flat | wish | catkin |
| **Syllables** | | |
| flat | wish | cat-kin |
| **Onset and rime** | | |
| fl-at | w-ish | c-at  k-in |
| **Phonemes** | | |
| f-l-a-t | w-i-sh | c-a-t-k-i-n |

These experiences will also have given them a firm grasp of the directional principles of English print (follow the words from left to right across the page to the end of the line, then start again at the left end of the next line down).

During Year 1, extended reading will introduce children to a wider range of print conventions. By the end of the year, they should be familiar with some of the distinctive ways in which information and reference books use print and illustration. Many children will be aware of features like an index or content pages, though they will continue to need help in using them.

Most children will be able to recognise a collection of whole words, including their own names and common words they see regularly in the world around them. The ability to recognise these develops from repetitive and purposeful encounters with such words. However, children will not be able to read them acurately and immediately until, helped by the teacher or another competent reader, they have seen the words read in a variety of situations. For example, a child who can 'read' the word *beans* from the label of a tin may not necessarily be able to read it when it is printed on a seed packet.

During Year 1, it is particularly important to check that children know the very frequent function words like *he, she, was, the, it* and so on. Many of these words are phonically irregular; they will not be supported by the non-verbal props which surround items such as brand names and street signs, and some of them may be difficult to distinguish from similar words (*if* and *it*, for example). By the end of the year, most of the children should be able to recognise instantly not onlu the 45 high frequency words suggested in the National Literacy Strategy for Reception but they should also be making progress in recognising more and more of the 100 or so words that make up 50% of this total.

For most children of this age, phonological awareness, or the knowledge that spoken words consist of smaller units, is at a transitional stage. To help illustrate this, the table below shows different ways in which spoken words and syllables may be analysed.

Because our writing system is based on the representation of phonemes by individual letters or groups of letters, it would seem to make sense to start to teach children to read by showing them the links that exist between particular phonemes and the letters that represent them in print. However, until children are aware that words can be broken down into phonemes, a teaching strategy like this is likely to confuse. The evidence suggests that, while many children at this age have only just begun to become aware of individual phonemes in words, (particularly single phonemes at the beginnings of words), the awareness of onsets and rimes is already well developed.

Thus, though most children will be able to hear the similarity between words like *fish, wish* and *dish* on the one hand (shared rime) and words like *fish, fall* and *foot* on the other,

(shared onset), some of them may find it difficult to isolate the separate sounds *fuh i* and *sh* in the word *fish*.

It is not surprising that children are more aware of onsets and rimes than of phonemes, since the types of language play (verses, jingles, tongue-twisters, alliterating names) that children of this age find so fascinating are generally based on rime or onset. Phoneme-by-phoneme awareness acquires most of its relevance when children begin to feel the need to spell new words. Writing activities, therefore, both shared and individual, supply the best opportunities to develop the children's ability to recognise phonemes.

A small number of children in Year 1 may already be reasonably fluent readers, while others will be able to read aloud from favourite story books, combining memorised phrases with a recognition of a number of sight words. With help, they may be able to identify new words by making analogies with known words. For example, if children are able to recognise the word *Mum*, and know that the *m* at the beginning of the word represents the *m* sound, this might give them a start in reading an unfamiliar word like *mouse*. Similarly, children who have been encouraged to note the sound/spelling similarity between known words like *sat*, *mat* and *cat* will have been given a very useful start when it comes to decoding an unfamiliar word like *splat*.

Reading is not, however, merely a matter of decoding words one at a time. Children usually meet words in sentences and stories. The overall gist of what has already been read, and the grammatical structure of the sentences within which unfamiliar words occur, provide children with clues which can help them to identify such words. Illustrations can also help. Most children of this age will need some help in co-ordinating all these different sources of information. Some children may rely too much on their memory of a familiar story, and make guesses which ignore the structure of the word. Others may be so intent on the structure of the word that they neglect to think about the meaning of what they have been reading. The great challenge for Year 1 teachers is to monitor the strategies used by these early readers, and provide appropriately differentiated guidance.

## Key area: Writing

Learning to write provides children with the challenging task of converting speech into visible, permanent form. In order to do this successfully, they need to become more aware of the components of their own spoken words, as well as of their printed equivalents. Thus, writing does not simply provide children with the skill itself, it should give them an enhanced awareness which will also help their reading.

The majority of Year 1 children can write at least their own names independently, forming and orienting the letters correctly. Although this might seem a small beginning, the insights into the writing process provided by this personal act of creation can be deeply significant. A child will be greatly attached to his or her own name and remembering its spelling teaches the importance of a fixed sequence of letters. Being able to produce this sequence at will gives a sense of competence and confidence. The association of a set of highly familiar letters with the even more familiar cluster of sounds which make up the spoken name provides a starting point for discovering words which share similar sound/spelling relationships (particularly words which alliterate with the name).

Above all, perhaps, the ability to write their name demonstrates to children the central purpose of writing, which is the placeholding of meaning. Seeing their names written in a variety of places (on labels, in the register, on books and letters home) will already have provided some experience of this. Participation in the shared composition of stories, reports and other useful and enjoyable pieces of writing may have deepened and diversified their understanding of this idea.

In their own writing, children will display further understanding of this concept by talking about what they want to convey before they start to write and while they are writing. This might be a story-like caption to a picture, a letter to a school visitor, or a report of a personal experience. Even though the message that they then produce may not be written conventionally, they should be able to 'read' it back. They should also be able to return to the piece of writing later and derive the same meaning from it.

By the end of the year, children should have created several types of writing ranging from lists and simple personal statements, to accounts of events and retellings or responses to stories. Although many of these may not exceed two or three sentences, and may have been supported by a framework which provided many of the words, this achievement (of a variety of completed works in the course of a school year) is an important step in the child's sense of authorship.

At this stage, children's writing is largely made up of talk written down. A variety of genres should be attempted (letters, reports, instructions, stories) though the finished products may often consist of a series of simple statements which relate events or list comments and observations. This demonstrates an awareness of the need to inform the reader, although children of this age have a limited understanding of how to take into account the perspective of the reader. They may, for example, use personal pronouns without first indicating the persons to whom they refer.

Syntactically, sentences are simple, as children's independent writing will not usually reflect the level of grammatical complexity they can achieve in speech. The vocabulary chosen will be from the child's everyday oral repertoire, though some pupils may import terms that they have come across when listening to adults or in books they have had read to them.

*PC Thoam is a yere nici.*
*man i thik He is ene way.*
*becas He let us in his van.*
*We takc abaoot it first.*
*then we went in it and we*
*had fun.*

*(PC Thomas is a very nice man. I think he is anyway because he let us in his van. We talked about it first. Then we went in and we had fun.)*

This sample of writing that Kerry produced after the police visit illustrates many of these points. Her writing is certainly informative, but nowhere near as detailed or as grammatically complex

as her oral retelling of the event. Her style is highly personal and conversational, and she makes no attempt to provide background information. Her sensible assumption is that the audience for this writing will consist of people who already know about the visit, so an explanation of who 'we' are, and how 'we' came to be talking to PC Thomas is unnecessary.

When writing is a new challenge for a child, the immediate, word-by-word demands of shaping letters and constructing spellings are the most compelling ones, and it is therefore inevitable that less attention will be paid to more general concerns like sentence structure and choice of vocabulary. It is therefore important to provide opportunities for shared, supported writing, where the teacher or another competent writer acts as a scribe, while the child or children, freed from immediate struggles with spelling and handwriting, focus on more strategic concerns.

Thus, by the end of the year, children should have been introduced, through shared writing, to aspects of writing that they may not be ready to use independently. These may include the use of more complex sentence patterns, adventurous vocabulary and simple metaphors and similes.

## Spelling

It is impossible to make any neat generalisations about the mixed range of strategies used by children of this age in their own attempts at spelling. However, the actual orthography used by a Year 1 child writing independently generally shows some awareness of letter/ sound relationships. Children whose spelling is at the pre-phonetic stage may use letter names instead of speech sounds, or produce letter strings which simply represent the most important sounds in the words that they are attempting to spell (for example, *KT* for Katey, *plesmn* for policeman). Children who have acquired more phonemic awareness often produce

strings in which all the sounds that they hear in a word are represented by one letter each (*cula* for colour, *scul* for school). Mixed in with these auditory-based attempts, there may be partially-memorised visual strings (for example, *siad* for said) as well as words which have been correctly memorised or copied.

Confident Year 1 writers, with appropriate guidance, feedback and instruction, will work their way steadily towards competence, but there are likely to be others who have become anxious about spelling, and they may refuse to take the risk of committing their words to paper without support to ensure that they get every word right first time. These children sufficient support to get their ideas onto the page, but at the same time they should be coaxed towards independence through various strategies, such as writing as much of a word as they know before moving on.

## Handwriting

By the end of Year 1 children should be able to form all the letters of the alphabet with reasonable clarity. Some children will still be reversing *s* and *z*, or confusing letters that look similar like *p, b, q* and *d*. In most cases these difficulties will be temporary ones that vanish as the child develops the stamina and dexterity to write at greater length. The distinctive roles played by upper and lower case letters will not yet be clear to many children. (Look at the way in which Kerry uses the H/h distinction in her writing: the capital is reserved for the personal pronoun 'he', as if for a proper name.) Some children may switch between these forms or prefer one over another in all positions. Others will use the upper case to escape from difficulties with orientation (using, for example, a capital B on all occasions to avoid the uncertainty of which way to position the lower case letter).

By the end of the year, routine handwriting activities and children's experience of upper and lower case letters in their reading will have led to a much greater awareness of these conventions, though the inconsistent use of upper and lower case letters in the world around them may continue to cause confusion.

## Punctuation

Punctuation is probably the transcription skill that develops most slowly. By the beginning of Year 1, children will have noticed these marks while they are reading and are likely to have formed some rough ideas about their purpose. Confident writers will already be experimenting with full stops, and making some interesting mistakes in the process. Kerry's writing suggests a transition point in her understanding of this mark. The first four lines all end in full stops, the first two lines of which are unnecessary. Younger children often believe that full stops mark the end of lines rather than sentences. However, Kerry's final sentence spans a line break and is correctly punctuated.

The failure to use full stops, or to place them correctly, does not mean that a child 'can't write in sentences'. Taking Kerry's writing as an example again, it is clear that 'underneath' the punctuation errors there is a perfectly coherent sequence of well-structured clauses. Kerry's difficulty is not in writing sentences but in learning the conventions that mark them off from each other. Her partially successful attempts to do this are very typical of a Year 1 child. However, although some children of this age will use no punctuation at all, while others have mastered the use of the full stop and are beginning to experiment with more sophisticated forms of punctuation.

By the end of the year most children will have sorted out the difference between a line and a sentence in their reading, and will be beginning to use full stops in their writing with greater confidence. However, inconsistencies and uncertainties will continue to occur.

# Practical ideas

For convenience, these ideas are grouped under the key areas of speaking and listening, reading and writing, but it is important to remember that the National Curriculum requires an integrated programme in which the different aspects of language are closely interrelated.

## Developing key areas

## Speaking and listening

The ideas given under the headings below outline specific practical activities that might be worked into a timetable, but do not fail to take advantage of general opportunities to involve children in purposeful speaking and listening during the school day. Don't underestimate the benefits of working with information and instructions, collaborative discussions, imaginative and dramatic argument (in both small and large groups, one-to-one or presenting to an audience).

### Impromptu talk

In addition to planned lessons and routines, there will be many occasions during the school day when children can usefully engage in more impromptu talk. These include:
- sending an oral message with a child to another adult (appointing a helper to check the accuracy of the message makes this more reliable and less worrying for the message-bearer);
- involving the whole class in songs and oral games (old favourites like 'Ten Green Bottles' and 'Chinese Whispers' are still very useful);
- encouraging the children to answer the register (preferably read out in random order) by giving a word beginning with a particular letter or related to a specific theme;
- asking children what they think, or know, about topical events in the local or national news;
- occasionally halting the work of the class so that an individual, or a small group, can share something that they have done;
- asking children to talk in pairs about what was done or learned in the previous lesson on this subject.

### Creating settings for talk

In their nursery and reception classes, children will have experienced 'home corners' or more diverse role-play environments like clinics, shops and cafés. In Year 1, it can be very fruitful to continue with this practice so that, over the course of the year, the children experience a range of opportunities related to different areas of the curriculum. The following simulations have all been used successfully with this year group.

- *The space shuttle and mission control.* An assembly of boxes formed the shuttle itself, which was provided with a ship's log, celestial charts, computers, instruction manuals and (most importantly from the point of view of speaking and listening) a radio link back to mission control. The latter was also made from boxes and was equipped with similar facilities as the shuttle, plus a bank of telephones from which the ground crew communicated the progress of the mission to press, politicians and the astronauts' families. Groups of three or four children took turns to serve in either centre.

- *A Caribbean market place.* Part of the corridor outside a classroom was converted into a set of three or four stalls, displaying an array of real and pretend fruit and vegetables. There were also scales, price lists and imitation Eastern Caribbean dollars. Children took turns to play customers and farmers, both groups exchanging a good deal of gossip as well as taking part in commercial transactions.

- *A garden centre.* This was an early summer project which added a role-play element to the real life, seasonal activity of sowing seeds, transplanting seedlings and tidying up the school garden. A customer information desk offered advice and a display of leaflets, while a wide range of gardening products could be purchased at the till. Certain conditions need to be fulfilled if these role-play environments are to provide effective

stimuli for talking and listening:
- the role-play should be linked to longer-term projects;
- helpers and older pupils, suitably briefed by you, should sometimes play with the children, to demonstrate the kind of talk that would be appropriate;
- monitor the use of the role-play areas to ensure that each child is given adequate time to play in them. When the class loses interest, create a new environment.

# Large group discussion

Traditionally, children in infant schools spend a few minutes each day telling their 'news' to the whole class and answering questions from the group and the teacher. This practice has sometimes been criticised as being too teacher-controlled, neglecting the needs of less confident children, and limiting topics of conversation to the trivial and repetitive. Time constraints also mean that most of the talking tends to be done by a small number of the more assertive children.

However, a regular opportunity to talk and to listen as a member of a large group can be highly effective in developing children's ability to assert themselves confidently as they convey and clarify information. Here are ways to adapt the traditional pattern.

## Talking about talk

Devote a large group session early in the school year to working out agreed rules for discussion. The children should be able to formulate simple guidelines such as: *Take it in turns to talk; Only listen to the person whose turn it is; Don't interrupt anyone.*

Discuss tactics for helping everyone to keep these rules. Mention ideas that have been used successfully by other classes (having a 'talker's chair' or an imaginary microphone that is passed from speaker to speaker, or a hat or some other prop which the speaker wears or holds) then ask the children to make their own suggestions.

As the term progresses, use some sessions to help children to monitor how well they are doing as speakers and listeners. Ask them *What makes a good listener?* and *What makes a good talker?* and help to draw up a list of relevant qualities. Your own conduct during sessions should, of course, provide a model for this. Speakers need

to be reminded that listeners may not have the background information that they do, and that listeners need to be encouraged to base their comments and questions on what the speaker has actually said, rather than jumping in immediately with personal information and anecdotes.

## Involve children in planning

Use class discussion time to make the children more aware of what they are going to be learning and how this learning will be achieved. For example, a discussion period at the beginning of the week could look forward to the activities that will be covered during that week. If your schedule is flexible enough, it's useful for children to formulate their own plans and make choices about the sorts of activities they will engage in.

At the end of the week, children could be asked to talk about what they think they have learned during the past few days. Their perceptions of the purposes and outcomes of their lessons can differ dramatically from those of teachers, so this feedback can be very instructive.

## Telling and retelling stories

Storytelling provides a chance for children to experiment with richer vocabulary and more complex sentence structures. Their command of literary language and rhetorical devices can often be very impressive. Encouraging them to retell true and fictional stories which they have heard at home or at school can be a very entertaining way to develop both their oral language and their social skills, and also gives you an opportunity to monitor these aspects of learning.

## Cue questions

Elicit personal narratives by the use of simple cue questions. *(What's the funniest thing that has ever happened to you? Have you ever been lost? What's the first thing that you can remember?)* Such questions are more effective if you relate experiences of your own before asking them.

## Retelling fiction

Fiction offers endless possibilities – telling favourite jokes, reporting adventures seen on television and in the cinema, retelling favourite stories told or read to the child in school or at home. Most children will be content to retell as

english

literally as their memories will allow, although some will delight in adding their own flourishes or in altering the plot.

## Listening actively

In both true and fictional narratives, the role of the listener needs to be an active one, and there are several strategies which encourage this. The most obvious is by participation in choral aspects of the story *(I'll huff and I'll puff...!)*. You could organise some retellings as group efforts, so that at certain points responsibility for the story passes to other members of the group (the sequence preferably unspecified beforehand). A general strategy is to ask the audience, before the telling starts, to try to relate unfolding episodes in stories to similar events in their own lives. In this way, awareness of certain universal themes in real life and fiction (losing and finding, overcoming adversity, virtue rewarded) can be developed.

## Making up stories

Remember too that large group work can provide an opportunity for children to make up their own short, oral stories, either alone or in collaboration with classmates. At this age, such attempts at

spontaneous composition are best as an optional extension of a previous discussion based on shared experience. For example, having read the story of *Jack and the Beanstalk*, you might ask, *What do you think would have happened if Jack hadn't bothered to keep his axe sharp? Let's carry on with the story as if the beanstalk hadn't fallen. Who would like to begin?*

## Tall stories

Eliciting 'tall stories' based on ridiculous exaggerations of personal experience is another possibility. After a traditional news session, for example, you might say, *Now that we've heard about the funniest things that happened to people at the weekend, let's see if you can make up something even funnier. Can anybody make up an adventure that didn't happen and couldn't have happened to them at the weekend?*

As with other stories, it's a good idea to ask listeners to stand by to continue the story if required.

# Small group activities

Though, of course, a child's actual performance as a talker or listener depends on a lot more than mere group size, a smaller group (of three to six children perhaps) provides the child with a more immediate, and perhaps less threatening, audience. The following activities show how speaking and listening can be developed across a range of curricular subjects.

## Listening, explaining and clarifying

Give small groups of children a picture or object related to the topic being studied. Use a screen so that initially only one or two members of the group can see the object. These children then describe it to the other group members who have to either draw what is being described, or guess what it is. They should also ask questions to clarify statements made by the describer. After an agreed amount of time the object should be revealed, and the group can then discuss the quality of both the description and the listening. The roles of talker and listener are then reversed for the next hidden object.

## Brainstorming and negotiating

Present the children with an unfamiliar object or

picture, or simply the name of a topic that you are about to investigate ( for example 'the weather', 'machines', 'farms' – the more specific the better). The children then have five or ten minutes in which to share everything that they know about the subject (while you, or other adult helpers, jot down on the board the children's responses as they occur). Then ask them to decide which two or three of their shared ideas are the most important (these can be highlighted or underlined). Alternatively, children can brainstorm questions about the concept, and make their selection on the basis of those that they would most like to have answered.

## Role-play

Follow up the reading of a suitable story involving two or three main characters with a dramatic reconstruction or development of short episodes from the story (or the entire story, if it is a brief one). Half of the group assume the main roles and act out the drama, observed by the others. This can be a simple dialogue or a more theatrical enactment involving costumes and props. At an agreed point, observers and actors swap places. The new actors then present either their own version of what they have observed, or a continuation.

## Presenting a personal opinion

From time to time, organise the children into small

groups to discuss an issue which is relevant to them and ask them to offer and defend a personal opinion.

Choose a topic which is of interest to the children and which is sufficiently familiar for them to offer an informed view. Here are some possibilities.

● Deciding which items of PE apparatus should be put out for the next lesson and/or how these should be arranged. (This can be done as a three to five minute preliminary 'buzz group' activity when the children are actually changed and assembled in the hall or gym.)

● Discussing options for how a completed piece of work should be displayed. (You will probably have to supply the alternatives yourself, but always encourage the children to think up some of their own.)

● Choosing what sorts of books should be bought or borrowed to replenish the classroom library.

● Solving more controversial issues of school policy: *Should parents' dogs be allowed in the playground at home time? Should playtime football be confined to particular days?*

## Talking about spoken language

Organise regular sessions in which children first of all listen to spoken language being used in a variety of different ways, and then talk about what they have heard.

This can be done in a large group, but it is probably more convenient if a group of four to six children sit in a listening corner with head phones to listen to the same tape and then share their opinions. For this type of activity a tape bank, built up with the help of other teachers, parents and children, can be invaluable. It might include:

▶ stories read in a variety of languages and a variety of accents and dialects of English;
▶ people of different ages and cultural backgrounds talking about their memories;
▶ recitations of various types of poetry;
▶ examples of different types of talk – news broadcasts, weather forecasts, stand up comedians, cartoon characters.

By sitting in on the discussions, you can assess the children's awareness of language diversity and their attitudes towards it. By joining in the discussion, you can introduce ideas and terminology appropriate to the standard English and language study components of the National Curriculum.

## Reading and Writing

In the sections below, activities have been organised under the National Literacy Strategy categories of text, sentence and word level work. Reading and writing are treated together within these categories. All of these sections should be underpinned by some general principles informing all your work in reading and writing.

● Convincing children that reading and writing are both useful and enjoyable. In order to do this, you need to show children throughout the school day that you use these activities yourself, both to get things done and to relax.

● Respecting children's differences. Because children have very different interests and capabilities, no one teaching method or set of materials will work for all of them. You need to monitor their personal responses to the reading and writing activities you provide in order to achieve a more individualised approach.

● Keeping parents informed. You need to establish ways of communicating with parents so that they know about the school's approach to reading (including details of how the reading scheme works), how and when to support reading at home (including procedures for dealing with difficult words and reading reluctance), and how to contribute to records of the child's achievements and problems.

## Literacy Hour

The teaching framework devised by the National Literacy Strategy *Framework for Teaching* is the foundation for the Literacy Hour which all primary schools will have adopted from September 1998. One hour a day is dedicated to the teaching of reading and writing, and involves a rhythmic transition from whole class teaching, to small group work, and back again.

## Working at text level

The sections below outline particular approaches which can be applied to other projects. Underlying these specific suggestions is an emphasis on shared book experience. A wide range of both fiction and non-fiction is now available in Big Book format. This can give a whole class access to the overall meaning of the book through choral reading, while subsequent guided re-readings can focus on specific features like sentence structure, items of vocabulary and sound/spelling relationships within individual words. Many books are also now available in CD format, which allows a similar range of opportunities to a smaller group working at a monitor, while also providing motivating features like sound accompaniment to the word-by-word highlighting of the text.

### Create a Big Book

The creation of your own Big Books, through shared writing, with you or a helper writing down the children's ideas, is an excellent activity. It provides an effective way of broadening reading resources, and at the same time demonstrates a wide range of writing skills: story structuring, choosing effective vocabulary, sound/spelling relationships, the use of punctuation and, after the first draft has been completed, editing and proof-reading.

Two of the main objectives of shared writing are to demonstrate the links between talking and writing, and to give children a sense of ownership over their reading materials, so it is advisable that children's own grammar and dialectal features should be put down as they occur. Whether or not they remain in the published version of the shared writing will depend on school policy, but this is an issue which should be discussed explicitly with the children. It is precisely this kind of discussion that provides children with opportunities to develop the knowledge about language set out under the National Curriculum's standard English and language study sections.

## A particular author

One effective way of encouraging children to appreciate a range of literary ideas is to spend a week or two concentrating on the work of a particular author. Ideally, the choice of writer should be made by the children, based on a book that they have enjoyed sharing as a class. Once the choice has been made, you should collect as many of the author's books as you can, make a display of them, and ask the children to detect anything they all have in common. From this starting point, a sequence of activities might develop.

● Pairs or groups of children select particular books to read (multiple copies would be useful here). Any reasonably independent readers might be encouraged to read their selections alone, while you select a book to read with the whole class. During discussion time, common themes and differences between the books should be explored.

● Children can collaborate on composing oral book reviews which recommend their choices to the rest of the class. The content of these reviews can be used to prepare a chart in which information such as theme, characters and setting is tabulated for each book.

● Common themes which have been identified may be linked to stories from other sources that the children have heard, read or seen on television. These can then form the basis for independent or shared writing.

● Children could choose a particular story to dramatise and present at assembly.

● Characters from the whole collection could be painted by the children and used for a display, which might also include examples of their own writing, (simple captions; descriptions; letters to characters).

● Help the children to write letters to the chosen author, incorporating appreciative comments, criticisms and questions. These can be sent off individually, or edited into a class letter. (Letters to authors can be sent c/o their publishers.)

The ideal culmination for such a project would, of course, be if the author could visit the school.

## Exploring fairy tales

● A good link with the oral storytelling discussed above is a class display of traditional fairy tales. A wide variety of versions of these tales is available and children may be able to bring books in from home. As with the author project (above), an initial display can be used to stimulate a range of reading and writing activities.

● Help the children to make a chart which highlights similarities between different fairy tales. It is particularly interesting to collect tales from outside the European tradition and to compare these with more familiar fairy stories. The children's librarian at your local library should be able to help you and, given advance notice, may be able to assemble a collection of appropriate books.

● Follow up oral retellings with shared or independent writing in which children create comic strip versions of the stories, accompanying a series of pictures with simple captions and speech bubbles;

● Suggest that children finish off stories in a different way to the traditional ending. This is often more effective if it is preceded by a role-play which begins just before a crucial point near the end of the story, so, as suggested earlier, encourage the children to act out the consequences of Jack losing his axe as the giant climbs down the beanstalk.

## Non-fiction

Look at the distinctive features of information books. Collect a set of information books related to a current topic including, if possible, one or

english

two aimed at a slightly higher age group. Invite groups of children to browse through them and to find as many ways as they can in which these books differ from story books. Listing these differences would make a good shared writing activity. This will give you opportunities to introduce children to differences in purpose and layout, and to explain specific features like contents, index, sub-headings and captions.

If you ask the children to grade the books, they will probably select the 'flashier' ones as their favourites. At this point it would be appropriate to introduce ideas like accuracy and ease of use, adding a little detail to the old adage about not judging a book by its cover.

Give the children about 15 minutes to browse through a selected book quietly and to try to learn as much as possible about its subject matter. Weaker readers might be paired with more able partners, or groups of readers might work with the teacher or another adult. Knowledge gained from this activity can then be shared with the rest of the class.

Sessions like this can form a routine part of introductory work on new topics, and can be followed up by visits to the non-fiction shelves of the library.

## Questioning non-fiction

In order to develop a questioning rather than a receptive approach to non-fiction, hold regular sessions in which children question published material before, after and during their readings. Prepare brief extracts from books at an appropriate level for the group, then try some of the following activities.

● Children make guesses about what the extract is likely to be about, based on its title, the illustrations, the identification of a few key words, and a reading of the opening sentence. (Reading here can either be independent or with support from a partner or adult.)

● Once children have identified the gist of the text, they ask questions which they think the passage might answer, then read it again, in search of these specific answers.

● Before reading the passage, children might make a simple chart, based on the questions, which can be filled in as the reading progresses. This chart can later be used as a blueprint for the children's own writing.

● Prepare a paraphrase of the excerpt with content based on the original, but different wording. Delete key words from it, then read it through with the children, pausing at the gaps and asking for suggestions. Their knowledge of the original should enable them to fill these gaps;

● As an occasional game, present the class with a non-fiction passage into which you have inserted irrelevant or obviously untrue material. Read this through with the children asking them to identify the inserted sections. More able readers could do this independently, striking out or underlining the words they think are incorrect.

## Work at sentence level

The activities outlined below are all designed to involve children in thinking about sentence structure, and how it can help with the identification of unfamiliar words while they are reading. They are also intended to help children to diversify the sentence patterns they use in their writing. Avoid trying to define what a sentence is – even professional linguists can't produce a satisfactory definition. In Year 1, it is better to try

to build up a feeling for what sounds right and what makes sense.

● Stories, reports and other items produced by shared writing can be cut into separate sentences, shuffled and reconstructed – the lines of familiar nursery rhymes provide a good starting point for this kind of exercise. Alternatively written instructions, the steps taken in preparing a recipe, for example, can be scrambled and then reordered. This also provides an informal way of introducing the use of pronouns to young children.

● You can then cut sentences into phrase groups and reassemble them one at a time, with the children identifying which word group should come next. When the original sentence has been rebuilt, scramble it again and see if it can be put back together in a different order. If so, has the meaning changed? Following this, sentences can be decomposed into separate words and then rebuilt.

● Particular verbs, nouns and adjectives can be deleted from sentences, and other words substituted. The children can then be challenged to identify whether or not the resulting sentence continues to make sense.

● Children can take simple sentences and find 'slots' in them where other words or word groups might be inserted to expand the sentence.

● Create well-supported opportunities for children to take turns at writing a simple sentence on a daily basis, perhaps by providing a weather chart with stem sentences relating to temperature, wind direction and strength, and rainfall for the children to complete.

● Encourage children to suggest (both orally and in written work) endings for stem sentences linked to their previous reading and writing. For example, *If I were the giant I would…* or *I would rather live in the city than the country because…* John Burningham's *Would You Rather* also provides useful starting points for this type of activity.

● Children could also use their knowledge of story to fill in blank speech bubbles in strip cartoons based on familiar stories.

● Children can begin to collect favourite sentences from their reading, perhaps beginning with particularly alluring story openings or effective final sentences.

## Punctuation

All of the suggestions above should provide opportunities to discuss the use of capital letters and full stops or question marks. These are the punctuation marks for Year One in the National Literary Strategy.

## Work at word level

As with sentence level work, the activities outlined below should, ideally, develop from work at text level, though there is no need to restrict activities to this.

● Maintain the children's awareness of rhyme, alliteration and onomatopoeia by getting them to build up word families which feature these qualities. They can then use their collections for oral and written composition of jingles and tongue twisters.

● Children could construct an individual vocabulary of words which interest them personally. These can be collected on cards and used for a variety of sorting and spelling activities.

● Compose orally, and then record in writing, a variety of class alphabets, such as an alphabet of names, of real and imaginary animals, favourite foods, places, books and story characters. Display the results as illustrated zigzag books or friezes.

● Help the children to write class dictionaries of words related to topics they are studying. These can be put into books, displayed as a frieze or incorporated into the topic display.

● A list of frequently-used words can be pasted into each child's writing book or folder. Then, when children writing individually need to have a word spelled, they can help each other by pointing to the word on the list. (Always encourage children to look at the word and write it as a whole after one 'good' look, rather than relying on somebody else spelling the word out orally, or on letter-by-letter copying.)

A useful activity, often begun in nursery and reception, is to give children frequent, diversified opportunities to shuffle and sequence letters (magnetic ones work best for this). It can also prove very rewarding to give each child in a group the letters of his or her own name. With a helper, they can then be encouraged to make comparisons and contrasts, to swap, substitute and pool letters, to compose nonsense words and real words. This is a particularly effective activity for less able readers, but suspend the shuffling activities until you are sure that children have very firm knowledge of the correct sequence for their own names.

## Individual reading and writing

In the majority of schools, the type of shared reading and writing experience already discussed will be complemented by sessions in which children read independently, either alone or to an adult. Books will usually be drawn from a reading scheme, or selected from a variety of sources and organised in a way that provides a gradient of challenge for children to climb at their own pace.

Children should be placed at an appropriate point on this gradient according to what they achieved in the reception class, but you will need to bear in mind that the summer break may have affected children's progress. Try to 'test run' each child on a selection of titles during the first weeks of term and adjust placements accordingly.

## Reading conference

The individual 'reading conference' in which children read aloud to an adult and talk about what they have read provides an occasion for the teacher or assistant to help the child to apply the skills taught by the activities outlined above. The best way of doing this will vary from child to child, based on what the individual actually does while reading with you. This combination of one-to-one monitoring and teaching is an intensive business, and even with daily half hour quiet reading periods, you cannot hope to give more than two or three children enough time and attention during each of these sessions.

## Common approach

Obviously, help from assistants such as parents and older children is vital here, but it is important that everyone involved in listening to children read independently takes a common approach to the support they provide and the form of recording used. You need to agree with your assistants how you will all help the children to:

▶ select books of an appropriate level;

▶ use phonic, graphic and contextual clues to deal with difficult words;

▶ move on from familiar books with a low level of challenge;

▶ talk about what they have been reading in order to express and refine personal responses;

▶ participate in monitoring their own reading progress in reading diaries or charts. Who records progress is a sensitive issue. In some schools, assistants record only the amount of reading that the child has done. Judgements about fluency, comprehension and strategy are made only by the teacher.

## Handwriting

Handwriting activities should be short, frequent and intense. Five or ten minutes a day in which children practise the formation of letters and common letter combinations is much more useful than a twice-weekly session devoted to 'writing up in best'.

The policy adopted by your school will affect how you handle this area, but it's important to remember that handwriting is a manual and aesthetic skill, so any activity which develops dexterity and pride in the visual appearance of their work is likely to be beneficial.

Artistic activities linked to the production of the children's own books are particularly valuable here, for example, observational drawing for book illustration, the design of book covers, and the use of repetitive hand writing motifs as decorative page borders.

# Assessment
## Speaking and listening

It is important, when assessing the oracy of young children, to defer judgement until you have compiled a record of the child's speaking and listening behaviour in various situations and with a range of other speakers over a period of a term or more. Assessments based on less than this may label reticent children as 'language deficient', or judge children who merely talk a lot to be good talkers.

The absence of evidence of an expected capability on a particular occasion does not necessarily imply that capability does not exist. If a child doesn't follow your instructions on a particular occasion, it could be that you have not expressed them clearly enough. Similarly, a child's inability to communicate at school may be caused by shyness, language difference, or failure to understand what is required, rather than by a lack of oral ability.

Informal, anecdotal and wide-ranging records of how a child talks and listens in a variety of classroom and other situations should be kept, supplemented by information from the child's family about the child's speaking and listening skills outside school.

Many teachers find that the most convenient way to collect this type of information is to keep a notebook with a page or two dedicated to each child. Leave this in a position where incidental observations, including verbatim remarks, can be jotted down. In order to build up a systematic picture, you could observe a small number of children each day. Over the course of time, these observations will help you to judge the children's progress in:

- communicating simple needs;
- participating in the recitation of repetitive patterns from stories and poems;
- responding personally to stories read aloud or shared with an adult during a reading conference;
- awareness of rhyme and alliteration;
- listening to, conveying and acting upon instructions;
- listening and responding to other children in group work;
- relating personal experiences and sharing personal interests;
- telling and retelling stories;
- asking questions about things that are difficult, interesting or puzzling.

# Reading

Try to organise a reading conference with each new child as soon as possible after he or she starts in your class. Make this relaxed and comfortable and ensure that the book to be shared is chosen by you and the child together. Aim to spend some of this time reading with the child, some of it listening to the child reading, and the rest of it talking about that particular book and about reading in general. As the child reads, make notes about the strategies being used (simple memorisation, attention to sound/spelling relationships, word length, pictures, context), and try to assess through discussion the child's appreciation and comprehension of the text.

After the initial conference, inexperienced readers should read with you, or with another competent reader, at least two or three times each week. Published recording systems such as the *Primary Language Record* (CLPE 1988) and *Progress in English* (RALIC 1995) provide useful formats and detailed guidelines for the systematic reporting and interpretation of

this information. Remember to use this time not just for assessment, but to teach children to apply what they have learned about context clues and sound/spelling relationships to the reading of books for themselves. You should also encourage children to make critical, personal responses to these books.

The reading conference probably provides the richest source of data on a child's reading progress, but a fuller picture should also include elements such as reading diaries; in which you and the parents write to each other about what the child is reading, and reading strategies; records of the types of book and other material that the child has enjoyed, and information on the child's own view of him or herself as a reader.

In addition to this general information you may find it useful to keep tick-list type records in which the child's growing familiarity with particular phonic elements and items of sight vocabulary is monitored.

You could also keep a cumulative record of children's alphabetical knowledge (the names, sounds and formation of each letter) and also a record of their ability to recognise commonly-used words. (The National Literacy Strategy has produced suggested word lists for each age group.)

# Writing

Much of what has been said about the assessment of reading also applies to writing. Observing children writing, and talking to them about their work should help you to construct a picture of their skills and attitudes. Dated samples of writing of various types can be supported by observational notes about the child's approach to the task, the level of help that was needed, and their own reflections on their work. The most important elements of a child's understanding of writing include whether, in writing or in talking about their writing, they show that they can:

- produce and read back a coherent set of ideas;
- understand that changes can be made to a first draft;
- use a variety of forms of writing, such as story, report of personal experience, letter, list of items for a particular job and so on;
- use some vocabulary specifically related to the purpose of the writing, perhaps simple technical terms, or more 'literary' expressions in fiction;
- spell common words correctly, or in a phonically plausible way;
- make independent attempts at spelling unknown words by using word charts, dictionaries, and so on;
- form both upper and lower case letters legibly and with reasonable ease;
- locate letters on a keyboard with growing speed;
- use capital letters where appropriate;
- use full stops to demarcate sentences;
- appreciate that particular forms of writing (recipes, personal letters, news reports) have distinctive layout features.

# Mathematics
## including Numeracy Hour

The teaching and learning opportunities that you provide in Year 1 should build upon the mathematical foundations children have acquired in their nursery and reception classes. This base is particularly important as all other pure mathematics (mathematical knowledge, skills and understanding) and applied mathematics (real-life, problem-solving investigations) acquired later in life will be grounded upon it.

During Year 1 children should begin to develop a firm understanding of mathematical concepts and to make the necessary connections between:

- mathematical symbols: for instance '+' and '=' signs;

- mathematical language: for instance *plus*, *add*, *equals*;

- pictures: for instance

- concrete situations: for instance *6 boys add 8 girls. How many children are there altogether*?

This chapter provides a scope and sequence of work for Year 1, with the focus throughout placed on the learning objective rather than the activity. This should help you to ensure progression and continuity.

Children need to be familiar and successful with the materials, language and activities for each learning objective before they start the activities related to the next objective. However, it should always be remembered that mathematics is not a fixed, linear, hierarchical discipline – it is cumulative rather than sequential. Although the learning objectives in this chapter follow a step-by-step sequence, the way you use them will depend upon the needs, strengths and abilities of the individual children in your class.

## Language

Children need to be encouraged to discuss their maths, for it is through language that they will truly be able to grasp the significance and meaning of what they are learning. When you ask children to talk about what they are doing and thinking in mathematics, they not only show you how much they understand, but they also clarify and develop their own understanding.

While it is important to accept children's early mathematical vocabulary, you should also teach them the correct, more formal, mathematical language as appropriate. For example,

when first learning about addition, children will probably use terms such as and, altogether, and how many, however, while you are talking to them, you can introduce terms such as add, plus and equals.

You need to be continually asking questions that will help them to:

* make connections in mathematics, such as the link between the current teaching and learning objective and that of previous objectives: *Do you remember our work on 2-D shapes last week? How does that help you to answer this question?*;
* develop a greater understanding of the learning objective, such as the link between the teaching and learning objective and the various mathematical activities: *What have you learned from the game you have just played?*;
* make new discoveries in mathematics, such as bring to their attention a new concept that is evident from the current teaching and learning objective: *What have you done so far?*;
* apply their mathematical knowledge to other contexts, such as money, shape, measures, other problems: *If we know that 13 + 4 = 17, what do you think 13p + 4p equals?*.

## Children new to English

There may be some children in the class for whom English is a second or other language (ESOL). This makes the job of ascertaining where they are in their mathematical understanding, and how and where to take them forward, all the more difficult. ESOL children need to be exposed to English mathematical vocabulary and symbols as soon as possible, but only after they have made the connection between the written and spoken mathematical language and symbols of their mother tongue with their English equivalents. There may be mathematical charts in community languages available in your area. If not, enlist the help of parents or older children who speak the language you need, to prepare charts with you. Unlike Farsi (shown on the chart below) many languages do use the same symbols as English.

You, or a helper, can 'read' the chart with children as they count in their mother tongue and you count in English. If you pair ESOL children with English-speaking children who have a good grasp of counting they can each learn to count in the other's mother tongue.

| 1 ١ | 2 ٢ | 3 ٣ | 4 ٤ | 5 ٥ |
|---|---|---|---|---|
| 6 ٦ | 7 ٧ | 8 ٨ | 9 ٩ | 10 ١٠ |
| 11 ١١ | 12 ١٢ | 13 ١٣ | 14 ١٤ | 15 ١٥ |
| 16 ١٦ | 17 ١٧ | 18 ١٨ | 19 ١٩ | 20 ٢٠ |
| 21 ٢١ | 22 ٢٢ | 23 ٢٣ | 24 ٢٤ | 25 ٢٥ |

## Estimation and approximation

Give children plenty of opportunities to estimate a rough answer to a problem, and approximate the range within which an answer is likely to occur. This will help them to develop a 'feel' for numbers and assess whether an answer is reasonable. The ability to estimate also plays an important role when children begin to measure with understanding. Real-life activities, such as cooking, sewing and building models, all help to develop this skill.

As children develop, encourage them to come up with an estimate as close to the actual answer as possible. Give them opportunities to do this in a variety of contexts, and with a range of materials and units.

## Linking concrete apparatus and mental mathematics

Children's first experiences of the world of mathematics should involve the use of concrete materials and real-life objects. Ideally, select items that are relevant and practical within their own lives for them to investigate and use. They will develop their understanding of mathematical concepts through manipulation of these everyday objects as this will enable them to see and touch the mathematics in which they are involved.

They will, however, reach a stage when they are ready to move away from manipulating concrete apparatus and begin to internalise their understanding – this is the real beginning of 'mental mathematics'.

Unfortunately, children don't give off a signal when this internalisation has occurred, so it is often difficult to know precisely when their need for apparatus has passed. It is only through observation, questions and discussions that you will be able to check whether they are ready to work without props.

● *You have just shown me that if you have seven pencils and you take away four pencils you will have three pencils left. Let's put the pencils away. Can you tell me what is seven subtract four?*

By the end of Year 1, children should be able to recall certain mathematical facts from memory. They should progress from having an understanding of addition and subtraction facts to 10, to being able to recall these facts instantly. This recall enables them to apply their mathematical knowledge of known facts (for example 5 + 3 = 8) to unknown or 'derived' facts (for example 65 + 3 = 68).

There will, however, be times when the children are working out problems and will need to return to using concrete apparatus. Ensure any apparatus required is available for them to use whenever they want it.

## Practical experiences

Practical learning situations (where children use concrete apparatus in real-life, problem-solving investigations) often require a considerable amount of time to organise. However, if the practical work is properly structured, with clear learning objectives, and is followed up by appropriate questions and group discussions, it is time well spent.

For many young children practical work provides the most effective means of understanding a particular mathematical concept. It enables them to think through the mathematics contained in the situation and develop a greater understanding of the learning objective which you are intending them to achieve.

# Children's recording

At the beginning of Year 1 the emphasis should still be on practical experiences and talking about mathematics. Children should not be required to write or copy mathematical problems.

Gradually, during the year, children will begin to want to record their results and should at first be encouraged to do so using their own methods of recording. Eventually they will need to use more conventional recording techniques and will need to learn to use the standard or formal methods of recording using mathematical signs and symbols, such as 3 + 4 = [ ].

# Numeracy Hour

During Numeracy Hour, all the children should be working on mathematics at the same time for the whole period. The mathematics you do in Numeracy Hour will not be a part of a general theme or integrated work, but should be focused on teaching specific mathematical concepts and methods.

You will be spending most of the time directly teaching and questioning the class. Children should spend approximately half of their time in a direct teaching relationship with you, and the rest of the time working independently either in groups, pairs or individually. Each lesson should follow this structure.

### Oral work and mental calculation (about 10 minutes)
Aimed at:
- developing mental fluency in previously-taught concepts/methods and developing children's oral skills (whole class).

### Main activity (about 25 minutes)
Aimed at:
- introducing children to new mathematical concepts/methods (whole class, group)
or
- consolidating previously-taught concepts/methods (whole class, group)
and
- providing children with opportunities to practise, consolidate, use and apply taught mathematical concepts/methods (groups, pairs, individuals).

### Plenary (about 10 minutes)
Aimed at drawing together the main teaching points of the lesson (whole class).

# What should they be able to do?

## Key area: Using and applying mathematics

When planning for Attainment Target 1 you need to provide children with opportunities to:
* use and apply mathematical knowledge, skills and understanding that have been previously learned, practised and consolidated, in problem-solving situations;
* acquire knowledge, skills and understanding through 'real-life', meaningful, problem-solving investigations.

Many children entering Key Stage 2 are still experiencing real difficulties in solving mathematical problems. This may stem from a lack of mathematical knowledge, or a failure to apply existing knowledge, but often these difficulties have more to do with lack of confidence and motivation, or an inability to persevere.

Give children the opportunity to apply their mathematical knowledge, skills and understanding in a environment which both motivates them and promotes the self confidence and perseverance they will need later in their primary school life to solve more sophisticated and challenging investigations.

By the end of Year 1, children should have had sufficient, appropriate experience to help them perform well in the following key areas. (In all cases the reference to 'children' refers to the majority of children.)

### Making and monitoring decisions to solve problems

Children should be able to:
* select and use materials appropriate for a particular task;
* select and use mathematics appropriate for a particular task;
* plan their work both mentally and using simple diagrams or pictures;
* check their work;
* complete a task.

### Developing mathematical language and communication

Children should be able to:
* make sense of a task;
* interpret mathematical information;
* talk about their work using simple language;
* represent their work using objects or pictures;
* record work simply.

### Developing mathematical reasoning

Children need to be able to:
* ask simple questions;
* make and test simple predictions and statements;
* use their experience to recognise and use simple patterns or relationships;
* make simple generalisations;
* begin to use logical thinking.

## Key area: Number

Children should be given opportunities to develop both individual and standard methods of

working; mentally, orally and written; in a variety of contexts, using a range of practical resources.

In order to ensure that children receive a broad and balanced range of experiences, offer them activities that employ the following tools:

- concrete materials;
- mental mathematics;
- paper and pencil;
- information technology.

## Place value

Children should be able to:

- count forwards to 100;
- count backwards from 100;
- recognise, read, write and order numbers to 100;
- recognise written number names to 20;
- count a given set of objects;
- make groups of objects;
- exchange units for tens;
- understand that the position of a digit in a number represents its worth, for example, 5 in 56 represents 5 tens;
- group objects to show the number of tens and units;
- recognise ordinal numbers to 20th.

## Money

Children should be able to:

- recognise all coins;
- use 1p, 2p, 5p, 10p coins in simple contexts;
- use combinations of coins to make amounts up to 10p;
- trade a number of 1p, 2p, 5p coins for a 10p coin;
- add and subtract amounts of money up to 10p.

# Methods of computation

## Patterns

Children should be able to:

- recognise patterns involving numbers to 100;
- count forwards in ones, twos, fives and tens;
- count backwards in ones and twos;
- copy, continue and devise patterns involving numbers to 100;
- make generalisations about patterns;
- make predictions about patterns;
- record observations.

## Addition

Children should be able to:

- understand and use the addition '+' and equals '=' signs;
- understand and use the vocabulary associated with addition, for example, *add, plus, total, and, sum of, more than*;
- understand number patterns in addition facts to 10;
- recall basic addition number facts to 10;
- solve basic addition problems to 10.

## Subtraction

Children should be able to:

- understand and use the subtraction '–' and equals '=' signs;
- understand and use the vocabulary associated with subtraction, for example, *subtract, minus, take away, difference, less than*;
- understand number patterns in subtraction facts to 10;
- recall basic subtraction number facts to 10;
- solve basic subtraction problems to 10.

# Solving numerical problems

Children should be able to solve numerical problems involving addition and subtraction facts to 10 in the context of real-life, investigative problems which involve:

- money;
- length;
- mass;
- volume and capacity;
- time.

# Classifying, representing and interpreting data

Children should be able to:

- sort objects based on given criteria using a Venn diagram;
- sort objects based on their own criteria using a Venn diagram;
- construct a block graph (where intervals increase by 1);
- interpret a block graph;
- construct a pictogram (where one picture represents one item);
- interpret a pictogram.

# Key area: Shape, space and measures

Children enter Year 1 with a practical understanding of their world gained from everyday objects, their own movement, and interaction with other people.

In Attainment Target 3, activities involving concrete apparatus provide opportunities for children to develop their spatial and geometric skills, knowledge and understanding.

## Patterns and properties of shape

### Patterns
Children should be able to:
- copy, continue and devise a pattern;
- make generalisations about patterns;
- make predictions about patterns;
- record observations.

### 3-D solids
Children should be able to:
- recognise and name a cube, cuboid, cylinder and sphere;
- sort known 3-D solids using a variety of criteria.

### 2-D shapes
Children should be able to:
- recognise and name a square, rectangle, triangle and circle;
- sort known 2-D shapes using a variety of criteria.

## Position and movement

### Position
Children should be able to:
- describe the position of an object in relation to themselves;
- describe the position of an object in relation to other objects;
- describe the position of an object in models, pictures and diagrams;
- draw a sketch from a model.

### Movement
Children should be able to:
- draw a path on a sketch to show a route followed;
- follow a route marked on a plan.

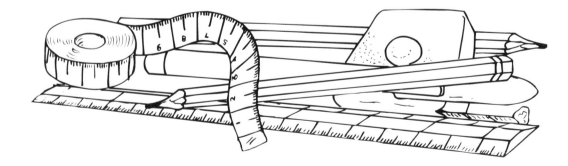

# Understanding and using measures

## Length

Children should be able to:

- measure the length and height of objects by direct comparison;
- measure the distance between objects by direct comparison;
- order length, height and distance of various objects;
- measure objects and distances using non-standard measures and uniform non-standard measures;
- recognise the need for a standard unit of length.

## Mass (Weight)[1]

Children should be able to:

- use a 'balance';
- measure by direct comparison;
- order the mass of various objects;
- use non-standard measures and uniform non-standard measures;
- recognise the need for a standard unit of length.

## Volume and capacity

Children should be able to:

- measure capacity and volume by direct comparison;
- order the volume and capacity of various objects;
- measure the capacity and volume of an object using uniform non-standard measures;
- recognise the need for a standard measure.

## Time

Children should be able to:

- recognise special times of the day;
- order events within a day;
- order events over more than one day;
- order events – past, present and future;
- use the names of the days of the week;
- compare the duration of two or more events;
- understand the concept of time passing;
- use non-standard measures, for example sand-timer, water clock;
- estimate using non-standard measures;
- use a calendar to describe the days, weeks, months, seasons and years;
- use 'o'clock';
- tell the time on the 'o'clock' and 'half past'.

[1] In the National Curriculum the term 'weight' no longer appears. It has been replaced by the term 'mass'. 'Weight', the amount of pull something exerts, is properly measured in newtons; 'mass', the amount of a substance, is measured in grams.

# Practical ideas

*Mathematics*

## Classroom organisation

The following practical ideas can be taught in different ways. Nearly all of them can be introduced to the whole class – perhaps when the children are sitting around you on the carpet. The activity can then be continued or completed by groups of either mixed or similar ability. Offer extension ideas to develop the activities for any groups who finish quickly.

Some other activities, particularly games, are suitable for children to play in pairs, while others can be worked on individually.

Under each main heading, the activities are ordered to reflect a natural progression, so you may choose to follow the sequence shown.

 ## Making a start

The first activities under each main heading are particularly suitable for introducing the concept.

## Assessment

Most activities can be used for some form of assessment. However, those that are particularly suitable for assessment purposes have the ○ next to them.

## Numeracy Hour

Many of the practical ideas which follow are suitable for use in the Numeracy Hour. For example, if you were introducing children to the number facts for 6, your Numeracy Hour could follow this pattern:

### Oral work and mental calculation
▶ Play 'Make six' with a dice (see page 57).

### Main activity
▶ Use interlocking cubes to demonstrate addition number facts for 6 (see page 57).

▶ Using real objects, children make addition number facts for 6 (see page 58) and write down the corresponding calculation.

### Plenary
▶ Ask individual children to share what they have been doing with the rest of the class.
▶ Discuss the main teaching points of the lesson.

## Using and applying mathematics

Whenever you undertake a particular investigation with your class it should always be based on your current mathematics topic, for example 3-D solids, length or time. This not only helps children to acquire new knowledge, skills and understanding but also enables them to use what they already know in a real-life, problem-solving situation.

## Number
## Understanding place value

### Counting 0–100

● Count round the room from 0–100.

● Count round the room from 100–0. As the next number is said, each child has to use a different voice for example soft, loud, scared, like a lion, and so on.

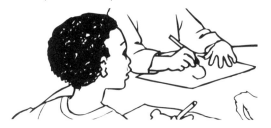

## Reinforcing 0–20

● Display number posters from 0–20 showing: number, number name, a group of objects.

● ✪ Children match a set of 0–20 number cards, number name cards and number picture cards.

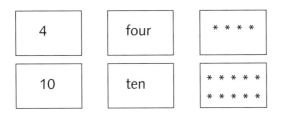

● ✪ Using 0–20 number cards and/or number name cards children make towers from interlocking cubes.

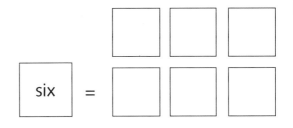

## Using 1-100 charts

● ✪ Count forwards in ones and count backwards in ones.

● ✪ Identify the patterns that occur: for example the pattern of 5s in the units column, the pattern of 2s in the tens column. See below.

● ✪ Using a large 1–100 chart, cover up one or more numbers. Ask the children to identify the number(s) that are hidden.

● ✪ Ask children, individually, to fill in an incomplete 1–100 square. See chart at the top of page 54.

| 1 | 2 | 3 | 4 | 5 | 6 | 7 | 8 | 9 | 10 |
|---|---|---|---|---|---|---|---|---|----|
| 11 | 12 | 13 | 14 | 15 | 16 | 17 | 18 | 19 | 20 |
| 21 | 22 | 23 | 24 | 25 | 26 | 27 | 28 | 29 | 30 |
| 31 | 32 | 33 | 34 | 35 | 36 | 37 | 38 | 39 | 40 |
| 41 | 42 | 43 | 44 | 45 | 46 | 47 | 48 | 49 | 50 |
| 51 | 52 | 53 | 54 | 55 | 56 | 57 | 58 | 59 | 60 |
| 61 | 62 | 63 | 64 | 65 | 66 | 67 | 68 | 69 | 70 |
| 71 | 72 | 73 | 74 | 75 | 76 | 77 | 78 | 79 | 80 |
| 81 | 82 | 83 | 84 | 85 | 86 | 87 | 88 | 89 | 90 |
| 91 | 92 | 93 | 94 | 95 | 96 | 97 | 98 | 99 | 100 |

| 1 | 2 | 3 | 4 | 5 | | 7 | 8 | 9 | 10 |
|---|---|---|---|---|---|---|---|---|----|
| | 12 | 13 | 14 | 15 | 16 | 17 | | | 20 |
| 21 | 22 | | 24 | 25 | 26 | 27 | 28 | 29 | 30 |
| 31 | 32 | 33 | 34 | 35 | | 37 | 38 | 39 | 40 |
| | | | | | | | | | |

## Using 0–100 cards

Children can put:

● ✿ a pack of jumbled 0-100 cards in order.

● ✿ all the cards with:
1 unit in one pile,
2 units in one pile,
3 units in one pile…

● ✿ all the cards with:
1 ten in one pile,
2 tens in one pile,
3 tens in one pile…

● ✿ all the even numbers in one pile, odd numbers in another pile.

● ✿ Remove a card from the pack, ask the children to find out which card is missing.

● ✿ Deal a jumbled set of cards to the class, then ask two children to come out to the front and each display one of their number cards( perhaps 46 and 67). Ask the remaining members of the class to stand up if they have a number which is in between 46 and 67. (They should each hold up their card so you can check it.) Repeat.

## Tens and units

● ✿ Use either Dienes apparatus or similar Base 10 material. If these are not available, use interlocking cubes made into towers of 10 to represent tens, and single cubes to represent units.

● ✿ Show 1 ten and 6 units to the class. Ask: *How many cubes do I have altogether?* Ask a child to show 16 using the number cards and number name cards. Repeat, using other numbers to 100.

● ✿ Show one of the number name cards and ask a child to represent that number with the Base 10 material.

● ✿ Ask children to compare the size of two numbers, one of which is displayed using Base 10 material and the other as a number card, perhaps 36 and 62. Ask: *Which number is larger/smaller? How can you tell?* Try with other numbers such as 52 and 25, 74 and 47.

● ✿ Count forwards and backwards in multiples of ten, for example 10, 20, 30, 40, …100. 100, 90, 80, 70, …0.

● ✿ Count forwards and backwards in multiples of ten from different starting numbers, for example 26, 36, 46, … 96. 93, 83, 73, …3.

● ✿ Ask a child to make a tower of 24 interlocking cubes, then ask a second child to add ten cubes so that it has 34 interlocking cubes. Ask a third child to add another ten cubes to raise the height to 44 interlocking cubes. Ask: *What do 24 and 10 make? What do 34 and 10 make? If we added 10 more* cubes, what would come next? And then ...? Discuss the pattern with the children (24, 34, 44, ...94).

● ☺ Display cards showing the multiples of ten: 10, 20, 30, 40, ...100.

● ☺ Remove a card, and ask the children to identify the missing number.

● ☺ Jumble the cards, then ask the children to put them in the correct order.

● ☺ Play matching games with the numbers from 0–20. Children, in pairs, can play Pelmanism with number cards, and number name cards. Some useful variations on this are:
❱ matching number cards and number picture cards;
❱ matching number name cards and number picture cards;
❱ using a selection of cards from 0–100.

## Ordinal numbers

● Using ordinal cards marked from 1st to 20th, hand out cards at random to 20 children. Give another child the challenge of placing the group in order.

● Set the cards beside groups of objects (perhaps counters) with a visible rank order. Ask: *If these were groups of sweets, which group would you choose first? And second? Put the cards beside the groups to show the order you would choose.*

● When the children are lined up, ask: *Who is third in line? Who is second from the end of the line? What position is Dalgit in the line?* and so on.

● During PE lessons encourage the childrens awareness of ordinal numbers by asking them to identify their own positions in the group, or places in the game.

## Money

### Recognising coins

Establish which children know all the coins. Arrange plenty of activities, such as matching, sorting and ordering coins, for those who don't.

● Place a selection of coins in a feely bag. Ask individual children to hold one coin through the bag and say what they think it is, without looking. They should then pull out the coin and name it.

●☺ Play matching games with coins. Shuffle a range of price cards (for example two each of 1p, 2p, 5p, 10p, 20p, 50p, £1), then spread them out face down on the table. Place the matching coins (two each of 1p 2p, 5p, 10p, 20p, 50p, and £1) in a feely bag. Children should take turns to chose a coin from the bag and place it beside one of the price cards. They then turn the card over and, if it matches, they keep it. If it doesn't match, they return it to the feely bag. The game continues until all the coins are used.

### Using coins

● Create a variety of shop types in the home corner so that children can play 'shops' using a full set of coins, and a collection of shop items labelled 1p, 2p, 5p, 10p, 20p, 50p or £1. One child should act as the shopkeeper, while the other children are shoppers. Shoppers choose an item and offer the correct amount of money. The shopkeeper then checks that the amount offered is correct.

● Encourage children to use a variety of combinations of coins for items costing 2p, 5p and 10p (5p = 2p, 2p and 1p or 1p, 1p, 1p, 1p and 1p).

● Progress by asking the shoppers to pay too much and the shopkeeper to give change for items costing up to 10p, *This shopper has given you 10p, and has bought an item costing 7p. How much change do you need to give?*

● Show the children how to make combinations of coins for amounts up to 10p, for example 6p = 2p, 2p, 2p or 6p = 1p, 5p. Demonstrate, then ask them to find other combinations.

● Encourage children to apply their knowledge of addition and subtraction number facts to solve money calculations with amounts up to 10p.

## Developing an understanding of methods of computation

### Patterns

● Children should be able to count forwards in ones, twos, fives and tens; and backwards in ones and twos.

● Use a 1–100 chart to identify the patterns that occur in the columns and rows.

● Identify the patterns in addition and subtraction number facts to 10, for example;

| | |
|---|---|
| 0 + 6 = 6 | 6 − 6 = 0 |
| 1 + 5 = 6 | 6 − 5 = 1 |
| 2 + 4 = 6 | 6 − 4 = 2 |
| 3 + 3 = 6 | 6 − 3 = 3 |
| 4 + 2 = 6 | 6 − 2 = 4 |
| 5 + 1 = 6 | 6 − 1 = 5 |
| 6 + 0 = 6 | 6 − 0 = 6 |

### Addition

● Using objects, number cards, number name cards and/or number picture cards ask: *Which number is one more?* Repeat this for different numbers, then extend it to 'two more than' or 'three more than'.

● Place five cubes in a feely bag, then add another two. Ask: *How many are there altogether in the bag?* Repeat this using different combinations of cubes up to a total of ten.

● ✪ Children can take turns to throw two dice, add the numbers together and choose the corresponding number card.

● ✪ Throw a dice and call out the number of dots on it, for example three. Then say: *Make eight.* Working in pairs, children should hold up the card that, when added to 3, equals 8 (for instance 5). Roll the dice again and repeat for other numbers. Challenge more able pairs with harder additions.

● Use interlocking cubes of two different colours to demonstrate addition facts for 3, 4, 5, 6, 7, 8, 9.
For example addition combinations for 5.

$$5 + 0 = 5$$
$$4 + 1 = 5$$
$$3 + 2 = 5$$
$$2 + 3 = 5$$
$$1 + 4 = 5$$
$$0 + 5 = 5$$

● Show addition calculations using a number line.
For example 3 + 2 = 5

```
|   |   |   |   |   |   |   |
0   1   2   3   4   5   6   7
```

(A number line from 0–7 with a jump going from 0 to 3 and another jump from 3 to 5.)

## Subtraction

● Using objects, number cards, number name card and/or number picture cards, ask: *Which number is one less than this?* Repeat this for different numbers, before you extend to two less, then three less.

● Count eight cubes into a feely bag, then take out three. Ask: *How many are left in the bag?* Repeat this, using different numbers of cubes up to ten.

● ✪ Children might take turns to throw two dice, subtract the smaller number from the larger number, then choose the corresponding number card.

● ✪ Throw a dice and call out the number of dots on it, for example 3. Say; *Subtract from ten.* Working in pairs, children hold up the card that shows the answer, for instance 7. Throw the dice again and ask them to make other numbers. Offer more challenging subtractions to more able pairs.

● Use interlocking cubes to demonstrate subtraction facts for 3, 4, 5, 6, 7, 8, 9.
For example subtraction combinations for 5.

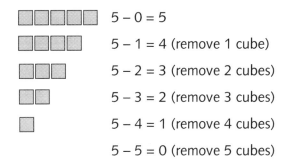

$$5 - 0 = 5$$
$$5 - 1 = 4 \text{ (remove 1 cube)}$$
$$5 - 2 = 3 \text{ (remove 2 cubes)}$$
$$5 - 3 = 2 \text{ (remove 3 cubes)}$$
$$5 - 4 = 1 \text{ (remove 4 cubes)}$$
$$5 - 5 = 0 \text{ (remove 5 cubes)}$$

● Show subtraction calculations using a number line.
For example 5 – 3 = 2

```
|   |   |   |   |   |   |   |   |
0   1   2   3   4   5   6   7
```

(a number line from 0–7 with a jump going from 5 to 2)

## Addition and subtraction

Children should work on addition and subtraction using all of the following real objects:
● mathematical apparatus, such as counters, cubes, Cuisenaire, Dienes;
● numbers, perhaps magnetic numbers or

number cards;
● number lines.

## Number facts

● ☼ Ask: *How many ways can you make five ?*
For example:
3 + 2 = 5
10 – 5 = 5
2 + 3 = 5
8 – 1 – 2 = 5
1 + 2 + 2 = 5
As a variation, use any number from 0 to 10.

● IT: Children can generate their answers on the computer for display.

● Use flash cards with addition and subtraction facts to ten to produce instant recall of number facts.
For example:

| 4 + 3 = | | 7 |
|---------|--|---|

front: 4 + 3 =  , back: 7.

● ☼ Ask the children to show examples of addition and subtraction facts to ten using real objects, for example: 7 + 2 = 9.

● Display all the addition and subtraction number facts to ten on a wall chart, for example addition number facts for six:
6 + 0 = 6
5 + 1 = 6
4 + 2 = 6
3 + 3 = 6
2 + 4 = 6
1 + 5 = 6
0 + 6 = 6

● Have a number fact of the day, for example 6+2=8. Ask each child to repeat it in a different voice: softly, loudly, terrified, happy, cross, like a cat, dog, and so on. At random moments in the day call out to individual children: *Manjit, what is six plus two? Tracey, what is two plus six?*

● Solving numerical problems. Children should be given opportunities to apply their knowledge of addition and subtraction number facts in a variety of contexts, including:
◗ money;
◗ length;
◗ mass;
◗ volume and capacity;
◗ time.

## Classifying, representing and interpreting data

### Classifying

● Sort objects using two non-intersecting circles (hoops, string, or circles drawn on large sheets of paper).
Criteria might include:
◗ large/small;
◗ square/round;
◗ blue/red;
◗ will roll/will not roll;
◗ makes a loud sound/quiet sound;
◗ long/short.

● Children should place objects into the corresponding circle. Any objects that do not fit into either circle remain outside both, for example objects that are neither round nor square.

● Repeat the activity using hoops or rope rings and the children themselves. Criteria for sorting might include: sex, hair colour, length of hair, eye colour, types of shoes, colour of clothes.

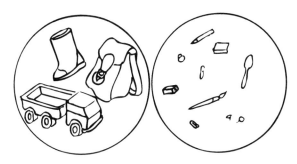

● Ask six children to choose two cubes from a mix of two different colours. Then prepare two intersecting circles (hoops, string or circles drawn on large sheets of paper) and label these with the colours you are using, for example 'blue cubes', 'red cubes'. Next, ask the children who are holding cubes to move into the appropriate circle.

● Discuss what happens to any children who have chosen a blue cube and a red cube. Agree that they should stand in the overlapping section of both circles.

● Repeat the activity, sorting either objects or children. Criteria you might like to try include:
◗ will bounce;
◗ will float;
◗ will fit inside a cup;
◗ brown eyes;
◗ long hair;
◗ shoe with laces;
◗ wearing a sweatshirt.

● ✪ Children can sort number cards, number name cards and number picture cards using a variety of criteria, such as:
◗ more than 4/less than 4;
◗ less than 6/more than 6;
◗ between 2 and 7/ not between 2 and 7.

Encourage them to sort according to their own secret criteria, then challenge their friends to work out what criteria were used. (This is a good extension activity for able children.)

## Graphs and pictographs

● Draw a blank block graph labelled with the names of four colours on a large sheet of paper.

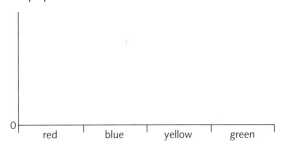

● In a feely bag place a (different) number of cubes of each of the four colours on the graph. Let each child select one cube. Next, ask one child to say the colour of his/her cube and then encourage all the children with that colour to stand up. Together, count the number, then choose a child to colour the corresponding number of squares on the block graph. Repeat this for the other colours.

● When the block graph is complete, ask questions that will enable the children to interpret the graph: *How many red/blue cubes are there? Which colour did we pick the most/least? Which colour was chosen eight times?*

● ✪ Make other block graphs in a similar way using, for example, attribute blocks, number cards/number name cards/number picture cards, dice (1-6) rolled 20 times.

● Draw a pictograph on a large sheet of paper.

● Let children pick a card from a shuffled pack of playing cards. Ask one child to say which suit his or her card is, then continue as for the block graph activity, drawing

pictures to tally the suits. When the pictograph is completed, ask questions that will enable children to interpret the graph: *How many hearts/spades are there? Which suit was chosen the most/least? Which suit was chosen seven times?*

● ☺ Children could make other pictographs in a similar way. Criteria might include:

● number of children with 0,1,2,3...brothers and sisters;
● favourite character in a story (selected from five characters);
● favourite food (selected from five popular food items);
● favourite pet (selected from five common pets).

● IT: Using a database package, demonstrate how to create simple block graphs and/or pictographs. Working in pairs, pupils might try inputting the data they collected in the earlier activities.

## Shape, space and measures

## Understanding and using patterns and properties of shape

### Patterns

● ☺ Individual children should be able to copy and continue patterns which use different attributes (for example, size, colour, shape) and discuss which attributes have been used.

● ☺ Children might devise their own patterns using different attributes. *Can your friend guess what pattern you have made?*

● Use a variety of objects to devise, copy and continue patterns, for example: Unifix

cubes, attribute blocks, shapes, counters, commercial pattern games, and everyday objects (shells, pasta, pencils, and so on).

### 3-D shapes

● Show children a cube, name and label it and discuss its properties in relation to faces and corners. Repeat this process with a cuboid, a cylinder, and a sphere.

● ☺ Encourage children to identify cubes, cuboids, cylinders and spheres in pictures and in the environment. Make posters (*Our cuboid collection*) on to which children can stick appropriate pictures they have found, alternatively set up some space for displays.

● Place a variety of 3-D solid shapes in a feely bag. Ask individual children to choose a shape and describe it while it is still in the bag. The rest of the class have to try to identify the shape from the description. The child then pulls the shape out of the bag to see if the class guessed correctly and, if so, places the shape beside the appropriate label.

● Play a game of *What am I?* Children describe the attributes of a shape or object and the class have to try to identify what it is.

● ☺ Children might sort a collection of 3-D solid shapes and everyday objects according to faces and corners.

### 2-D shapes

● Draw a square on the board or a large piece of paper. Name and label it. Discuss its properties in relation to sides and corners. Then repeat this for rectangle, triangle and circle.

● ☺ Challenge children to identify squares, rectangles, triangles and circles in pictures, and in the environment. Make posters and/or space for displays.

● Play matching 2-D shapes games. Shuffle a variety of 2-D shape cards (for example 4

× 5 squares, rectangles, triangles, circles). Children, in pairs, can then use these to play Pelmanism. To vary this, use irregular as well as regular squares, rectangles, triangles and circles. ('Irregular' squares are those standing on one of their points and 'irregular' circles are shown as ovals.)

● Provide square, rectangle, triangle, circle, picture cards and label cards (two of each), ask children to match the picture cards to the label cards.

● ✪ Children sort a collection of 2-D shapes (regular and irregular) according to faces and corners.

● IT: Using a simple art package, children can create their own 2-D shapes and 2-D shape patterns on the computer.

# Properties of position and movement

## Position
● Discuss simple vocabulary to describe the position of an object, and encourage the children to use it:
▷ in relation to themselves;
▷ in relation to other subjects;
▷ when describing models, pictures and diagrams.

The type of vocabulary that will prove useful includes: *near, close, far, to the left, to the right, in front of, behind, beside, next, next to, above, across, around, after, back to back, before, bottom, centre, close, down, up, far, first, forward, further, from, here, high, in, inside, into, last, low, middle, near, on, onto, on top of, outside, over, past, right over, round, side by side, there, through, top, turn, under, underneath, upside down.*

● Children could draw a sketch of an object (for example a teddy, an open book on its end, a LEGO model) which is on a table in front of them.
Now ask them to imagine they are standing behind/to the left of/to the right of the model and to draw a second picture of the object from that position. They should then stand in the suggested position to check the accuracy of their drawing.

● Children, in pairs, could play 'Copy my model'. Each child starts with the same number of LEGO bricks of the same colours and sizes. They sit back to back while one child puts pieces of LEGO together to make

a model. When this is completed, he or she describes the model in detail to the other child, who then has to try to copy it exactly, without looking. Once both children are satisfied with their models they should compare them, and discuss their similarities and differences. They then reverse roles and repeat.

● IT: Use a Roamer/Turtle/Logo package to describe position.

### Movement

● Provide children with simple plans of the inside of the school, then ask individual children to go to a specific place. (Remember to make a note of which routes you give to which children!) *Walk out the classroom door, over to the boys toilet, through the corridor to the office, across the hall, around to the door of Mr Simpson's room and back to our room. Draw a line on your map to show the route you followed.*

● As a variation pupils could be asked to draw a route, then to go and walk it, or to draw a route for their friend to follow. *Go with him. Did he follow the route correctly?* Provide children with a route marked on a plan and ask them to follow it.

● IT: Use a Roamer/Turtle/Logo package to describe movement.

## Understanding and using measures

### Length

● Hold up various pairs of objects, such as pencils, ribbons or paintbrushes, then ask: *Which is longer? Which is shorter?*

● Ask children to make long and short objects from Plasticine.

● Compare the distance between various objects, perhaps the door to the cupboard, or the door to the teacher's desk. Ask: *Which distance is longer? Which is shorter?*

● Compare the height of various children. Ask: *Who is shorter? Who is taller?* This can also be done using various objects, such as tower cubes, sticks or boxes.

● Measure the length of a desk using pencils.

● Measure the distance between the door and the cupboard using paces.

● Measure the height of a child using crayons.

● Children should experience a variety of measuring activities. They can:
▷ measure the length, distance and height of various objects in the classroom using Unifix cubes, pencils, and so on;
▷ order various objects according to their length and height;
▷ order the distance between various objects;
▷ predict length, height and distance;
▷ measure the length of a desk using their palm span.

● Ask individual children (with different palm spans) to tell how many palm spans long their desk is. This will lead into discussion of problems with measuring in spans, such as different size spans, distance remaining if not exactly a span (for example 3.5 spans).

● Measure other objects such as the board, the height of a table, the height of a child or teacher, and the length of the classroom using spans, feet, steps, and so on as units of measure. *Why do some people get different results?* Discuss the need for a standard unit of measure to resolve the problems of measuring with non-standard units.

● Introduce the metre rule as an instrument for measuring in a standard unit. The children can estimate, then measure, how many of their handspans, foot lengths and so on will fit into a metre.

## Mass (Weight)

● Ask children to feel objects of different mass, perhaps a feather and a bag of flour. *Which is heavier? Which is lighter?*

● Children can be challenged to find objects which are light and heavy. *Find some objects that are lighter/heavier than this book.*

● Show the children a balance and how it works, then ask: *How many blocks will we need to put on to balance this orange?* Pass the orange around the class asking the children to feel how heavy it is. Then pass a block around the class, encouraging the children to think about how many blocks will be needed to make the same mass as the orange. Write some of the children's estimates on the board. Place the orange on the balance, then count blocks onto the balance. When the balance is level, stop counting.

Repeat this, weighing other objects, perhaps a toy car, a doll, books, a pencil-case, or a shoe.

● Children should order the weight of various objects. As a class, discuss weighing very light and very heavy objects. Try to weigh a feather on a balance using blocks. Then try to weigh a brick on a balance using blocks. Discuss the need for a standard unit of measure.

● Introduce the children to the standard measure – gram (g).

## Volume and capacity

● Using containers of different sizes and shapes (shampoo bottles are useful), ask children to suggest which container holds most/least water or sand. After they have estimated, they should check their answers in a variety of ways.

Let the children try:

▶ filling one container and transferring its contents into the others;

▶ filling each container, using the same small container, and counting how many fills each will hold;

▶ filling all the containers and tipping the contents into identical containers for comparison.

They can then order the containers.

● Take three identical containers. Fill one full of water, another half full and leave the third empty. Ask the children to describe the amount of water in each container.

This activity can be repeated using sand, marbles and so on.

● Pour water from a jug into a small container until it overflows.

Ask: *Which holds more water, the jug or the container?*

● Children can measure a range of containers by filling them with various objects (observing the amount of space occupied by objects and comparing).

● Children can then place the different containers in order by observing the amount of space occupied by the objects, such as cubes, marbles or threading beads, and comparing.

● Ask children to build models using a variety of materials, (Unifix, LEGO, wooden blocks) then count the number of blocks they have used in their model.

Discuss the various models that have been made using the same number of unit blocks. Choose a simple model and ask everyone to copy it closely, using the same number of blocks. Repeat using other objects.

● Discuss the non-standard nature of:

▶ different-sized containers;

▶ the number of objects in a container;

▶ the number of objects in a model.

## Time

### Time vocabulary

● Discuss with the children the concept of time using the following vocabulary: *daytime, night-time, yesterday, today, tomorrow, all day, a long while, a little while, morning, afternoon, evening, night, now, later, before, after...*

### Routine and events

● Discuss the daily routine: in the morning before school, at school, when they leave school in the afternoon...

● Discuss and order:

▶ the events of the day;

▶ events over more than a day;

▶ events over a week;

▶ events past, present and future.

### Days of the week

● Introduce the names of the days of the week. As a class, fill in a chart identifying specific things that happen at school on certain days of the week. Illustrate it to help remind children of events in which they take part each day

● Children should be able to order a set of cards with the days of the week written on them.

### Measuring time

● Measure time using various non-standard measures, such as a sand timer or water timer. Ask: *How many times can you skip/ write your name/jump/put your hands on your head before the timer finishes?*
Using a 1-minute sand timer: *How high a tower can you make using cubes?*
How many books can you stack into a pile?

● Work out the length of time between two or more events.

### Months and seasons

● Introduce the months of the year using a calendar. Discuss the names of the months, the names of the days and their weekly cycle, the number of days in each month.

● Mark on the calendar:
▷ special national events;
▷ special school events;
▷ special celebrations;
▷ birthdays of children in the class.

● Label the four seasons on the calendar. Discuss:
▷ when they occur;
▷ differences between them;
▷ particular things that occur in different seasons.

● Discuss events that are significant to the children:
▷ this year (*This year you started in Year 1.*);
▷ last year (*Last year you had Miss Henry as your teacher.*);
▷ within their lifetime (*In 1996 the new supermarket was opened.*);
▷ next year. (*Next year most of you will have your seventh birthday.*).

### Telling the time

● Show the children an analogue clock and talk about clocks.

● Count the numbers.
● Talk about the 'hands' on a clock.
● Introduce the concept of 'o'clock'.
● Talk about important times of the day that feature o'clock and ask the children to draw pictures to show what happens at these times of the day.

● Beside each picture they should:
▷ draw the hands on a stamped clock face to show the time;
▷ write the time in words, for example 9 o'clock;
▷ write the time in digital time, for example 9.00;
▷ Introduce 'half past'.

● Show an analogue clock set at 4 o'clock, then move the minute hand to stop at the 6. Say: *This is half past four. It is half way round the clock.*

● Show a digital clock, also set at 4 o'clock. Change the time to 5 o'clock. Set the display to 4 o'clock again. Then advance the time to show 4.30. Tell the children: *This is 4.30, or half past 4.* The activity can be repeated using other times.

● Using both an analogue and a digital clock:
▷ show children times (o'clock and half past) and ask them to identify the time;
▷ ask children to show a particular time on the clock;
▷ set a time on a clock hidden from the children, then give clues: *It is after 3 o'clock*

or *It is before 4 o'clock.* Children have to guess the time on the clock. (This activity can be repeated in pairs.)

● Children might make their own analogue clocks and use them to show various times (both o'clock and half past). They can take turns at testing each other's knowledge of times.

● Play time-matching games. Working in pairs, children shuffle and play Pelmanism with time cards showing analogue o'clock-times in written and clock-face forms. To vary this, use pairs of cards of analogue and digital times in written and clock-face forms for o'clock and half-past times. Challenge able children with the more difficult combinations.

## Assessment

Children demonstrate the outcomes of their learning through speaking, writing, drawing and many other activities.

A variety of assessment strategies is necessary if you are to understand each child's stage of learning and how best to further develop that learning. Whatever assessment strategies you use, it is important to ensure that tasks are appropriate to the individual child and that they are directly related to the learning objectives. Activities marked with a ○ in the Practical Ideas section are all suitable for assessment purposes.

The levels of expectation suggested on pages 47 to 51 under the heading 'What should they be able to do?' provide a comprehensive checklist for assessing children's learning at the end of Year 1.

# Science

The National Curriculum specifies the science that must be taught at Key Stage 1, but individual schools still have to decide on an order in which to teach it.

The Orders for Key Stage 1 are divided up into seven units of work over a six-term period. As it would not be practical to cover every possible combination of units, the following programme for Year 1 is suggested:

## Programme

|  | Autumn Term<br><br>Unit 2 | Spring Term<br><br>Unit 4 | Summer Term<br><br>Unit 6 |
|---|---|---|---|
| Year 1 | Life Processes and Living Things<br><br>**2** Humans as organisms<br><br>**4** Variation and classification | Materials and their Properties<br><br>**2** Changing materials | Physical Processes<br><br>**2** Forces and motion |

If your school has allocated the units differently, you may want to draw on the ideas in the Year 2 book where Units 3, 5, 7 and 1 are covered.

If you follow this programme, you will ensure that in each year of Key Stage 1 every child will cover work within all three of the knowledge and understanding Attainment Targets.

*Life Processes and Living Things* has been chosen as a starting point because it provides a number of opportunities for simple introductory investigations. In addition, it appeals to young children's overwhelming interest in themselves! This unit contains a great deal of work and you may well need the longer autumn term in order to complete it.

*Materials and their Properties* introduces the children to the various ways in which materials can be changed, a topic which lends itself readily to simple investigative work, while *Physical Processes* introduces simple ideas on forces and movement, basically the way in which movement can be brought about and stopped by pushes and pulls. Much of this work can be carried out in the school grounds – if weather conditions permit.

It is, however, important to remember that there is no set order for teaching these topics. You can also add to or adapt them to suit your own needs and those of the children in your class. As long as all the units are covered at some point in Key Stage 1, then the statutory requirements will have been met, children will have covered the appropriate work, and will therefore be able to undertake the assessment at the end of Year 2.

# What should they be able to do?

The statutory Orders for Science are set down in four sections. At first glance it would be easy to believe that the three sections dealing with knowledge and understanding put the emphasis on the content of science rather than the process. This notion is soon dispelled by the realisation that *Experimental and Investigative Science (Sc1)* is regarded as having an importance roughly equal to the other three science sections combined. Although it requires no specific learning of facts, Sc1 will only be achieved over a period of time, perhaps the whole of the primary school stage, or even longer. The aim is for children to develop an understanding of scientific phenomena through systematic and practical exploration and investigations.

The National Curriculum identifies three components within scientific investigations. These are: Planning experimental work; Obtaining evidence and Considering evidence.

## Planning experimental work

Young children have enquiring minds and great curiosity about everything around them. It comes naturally to them to try things out, to see how things work, to manipulate, to touch and feel, to ask questions and seek answers – all attributes of a good scientist.

Planning includes asking questions and predicting. It is, therefore, important to provide plenty of opportunities that promote discussion between the children themselves, and between you and the children. Encourage them to ask questions of the *Who? What? Where? When? Why? How many? How much? How far?* variety. Children will not automatically come up with ideas that can be investigated unless they have had practice and have begun to develop an idea of what constitutes a scientific investigation.

In Year 1, the children's predictions will often be a guess, not based upon any scientific knowledge or analysis. Only when they have had some experience of appropriate investigations, activities and discussion will they acquire a basic scientific knowledge and learn to make predictions that are based on this, and on the data they have collected.

## Obtaining and considering evidence

Children should be encouraged to use all their senses to help them measure and record accurately. Most children in Year 1 will be limited to describing the simple features of the objects, living things and events they observe.

Considering evidence involves children in interpreting the results of their investigations and evaluating the scientific evidence. Encourage them to make comparisons, to look for patterns and to communicate their findings in a variety of ways. This allows them to share their thinking and to relate their understanding to scientific knowledge. In Year 1, most children's consideration of evidence will be limited to communicating findings in simple ways such as talking and drawing pictures. Some children may be able to progress to constructing simple tables or graphs.

## Knowledge and understanding

The three sections of the Programme of Study dealing with knowledge and understanding are: *Life Processes and Living Things (Sc2); Materials and their Properties (Sc3)* and *Physical Processes (Sc4).* These are instantly recognisable as the biology, chemistry and physics of secondary school days. (Bear in mind that the Programmes of Study are not always intended to show progression, and the letters a, b, c and so on should not be taken to imply increasing complexity.)

## Is there an Sc0?

There is a fifth area of the science curriculum which has no distinct title. Since it is supplied as an introduction to each key stage description, some people call this preliminary area Sc0. This fifth area applies across *Experimental and Investigative Science*, *Life Processes and Living Things*, *Materials and their Properties*, and *Physical Processes*. It consists of five parts and, incidentally, highlights many important cross-curricular aspects of science. Children should be introduced to these five components during Year 1, although there are few opportunities at this early stage to examine the work of great scientists, with the possible exception of Galileo's studies on falling objects (page 79) and, possibly, the story of Newton's discovery of gravity. Their are five parts in Sc0:

1. **Systematic enquiry** includes giving children opportunities to ask questions and to use firsthand experience and simple secondary sources to obtain information. It also covers the use of Information Technology.

2. **Science in everyday life** requires the children to relate their understanding of science to their own health and the environment.

3. **The nature of scientific ideas** is an opportunity to look at the life and work of great scientists and examples of scientific thinking.

4. **Communication** teaches children about appropriate ways to record and communicate scientific understanding.

5. **Health and safety** deals with children following simple instructions to control the risks to themselves, as well as recognising hazards and risks when working with materials and living things.

# Practical ideas

*Science*

## ❀ Making a start

The following ideas are just a few of the many ways you might introduce the three units (Units 2, 4 and 6) suggested for Year 1. Other suggestions are made in the 'Ideas bank' on page 80.

### Parts of the human body

● Show the class a cardboard cut-out, a shop dummy or some other model of the human body. (You can draw around a child lying on the floor on a large piece of paper to create a life-size outline. Arrange your model with one arm and leg bent to show joints and draw in some features.) Challenge the children, in turn, to place labels on the main external features of the body *(ankle, arm, body, elbow, fingers, foot, hand, knee, leg, toes, heel, knuckles, neck, shoulder, waist, wrist, cheek, chin, ear, eye, forehead, hair, mouth, nose)*. An alternative approach to this would be to put the labels on the 'body' in the wrong places, then let the children take turns to move the labels to the correct places.

● Play the game 'Simon says' or sing the songs 'Heads and shoulders, knees and toes' or 'Dry bones'.

### Variation and classification

● Children should gather information about their heights, weights, hand spans, arm spans, length of legs, length of feet (or shoe sizes) and so on. A series of simple block graphs could be produced for display around the classroom. Ask the children what titles the graphs should have.

The children can also compile an information file about themselves and possibly enter the information onto a simple computer database. *Do any of you have exactly the same measurements?*

● Collect some leaves from plants which show great variation such as the common oak, ivy or dandelions. Let the children examine several leaves of the same species to see how they differ in size, shape and colour. They should choose leaves of the same species which show the

greatest degrees of variation and produce tracings or rubbings, which can then be coloured and cut out. (Remind them to wash their hands thoroughly after handling the leaves.) Use the tracings or rubbings to make a display.

## Changing materials

● Put an ice-cube on a saucer and ask the children to watch it closely: *What is happening to the ice-cube? Why is it happening? What will happen next?* Can the children predict what will happen if some ice-cubes are placed on a sunny windowsill or near a radiator and others are put in the refrigerator or some other cool place? Let them draw what they see.

● Ask the children to warm some play dough or Plasticine in their hands. Put some in the refrigerator and look at it again later. *What differences do you notice?* Can the children see that the malleability of the play dough or Plasticine changes with temperature? *What happens to the cold play dough or Plasticine when it is warmed again? Are the changes permanent?* Encourage the children to write two or three short sentences to record their results.

● With the help of an adult, the children could warm up some jelly cubes or small squares of chocolate. Pour the liquid jelly or chocolate into an ice-cube tray and then put it in the freezer. After a while, take the ice cube tray out of the freezer and note what has happened. Can the process be reversed? Introduce the terms 'warm', 'cold', 'melt' and either 'solidify' or 'turn solid', then encourage the children to use these words in short sentences when they write down their findings.

## Forces and motion

● Collect together pictures of some toys or simple machines that are normally moved by pushing (such as a spinning top, a bicycle, a swing, a wheelbarrow or a supermarket trolley) or pulled along (such as toy animals fitted with wheels). Let the children decide whether each object needs to be pushed or pulled (or both) to make it move forwards. They can record their results in a simple table with two columns headed 'Pushing' and 'Pulling'.

● Provide a ramp (a short plank with a thick book

under one end) for the children to observe how wheeled toys travel down it. *If the ramp is raised slightly, do the toys travel faster or slower? How can the toys be made to change direction? Do they need a push or a pull? What makes the toys slow down and stop?*

● Working in the school hall, or on a playing field, provide a supply of footballs or other large balls. Let the children decide whether pushes or pulls are needed to make the balls start rolling. *How can the balls be made to roll faster or slower? How can they be made to change direction?*

# Developing key areas

# Life processes and living things

## Humans as organisms
### Food and drink

● Prepare a large chart, or a photocopiable sheet. Ask the children to draw pictures of their favourite food and drink on small squares of paper which can then be transferred to the large chart to form a pictogram. Alternatively, use a simple computer database (such as *Our Facts*, *Easy Works*, *Find IT*, *Datashow* or *Sparks*) to find the favourite and least favourite foods and drinks.

● Read the story of *The Very Hungry Caterpillar* by Eric Carle (Puffin). Ask the children what they would have chosen to eat and drink if they had been the hungry caterpillar. *Why would you have chosen these things? Why do we have to eat and drink?*

### Exercise and diet

● Ask the children to discuss how they feel after exercise. Consider, and perhaps make measurements of, the heartbeat, breathing rate and skin temperature before and after exercise. A simple stethoscope for listening to the heartbeat can be made by fitting a small plastic funnel into each end of a short length of rubber or plastic tubing. Children might count the number of

heartbeats in one minute. Breathing rate can be measured by letting each child place his or her hands on the lower part of the chest and counting the number of movements in one minute – often the rate of breathing doubles after exercise. (Children who suffer from asthma, bronchitis or other breathing problems should not attempt this activity.)

Skin temperature is best measured with a plastic 'fever strip' or a digital clinical thermometer if one is available. If not, ask the children to simply say whether they feel hotter or cooler after exercise. Explain to them, in simple terms, that during exercise we need more energy, so our heart pumps extra food and oxygen from the air to the muscles where the food is 'burned' chemically to produce the extra energy we need.

Discuss how, as well as providing energy for movement, foods also help us to grow, repair damage and keep warm.

## Medicines

Read *George's Marvellous Medicine* by Roald Dahl (Puffin) or *Going to the Doctor* by Anne Civardi (Usborne) to the children. *Have you ever had to take medicine when you were sick? What sort of illnesses have you taken medicines for?* Discuss the safe use of medicines, why medicine bottles often say 'Keep out of reach of children'

and what they should do if they find any medicines. Discuss other substances that should not be swallowed. The safety aspect could perhaps be reinforced by making a display of (clean) medicine bottles and other medicine containers with a suitable caption which the children can help to compose.

## Humans have babies

Ask a parent with a new baby (perhaps one aged three to six months) to bring him or her into the classroom. Let the children discuss with the parent when and what the baby eats, how long the baby sleeps, and any other aspects of care that interest them. The parent may be able to bring in photographs that show how the baby has grown and changed since birth.

The children could use photographs, and perhaps birth weights and lengths, to show how they have changed over the years. (Remember, however, that not all children will have access to photographs and information of this kind.) Discuss with the children how they expect to change as they grow up and grow old.

## Human senses

This part of the unit lends itself to a wide range of activities and investigations.

## Touch

● Make 'feely pictures' by sticking objects and materials with different textures onto card. Challenge the children, with their eyes closed, to identify the objects and materials by touch alone.

● Make a 'feely' box, then let the children take turns to identify unseen objects by touch. (Clearly all the objects used must be safe to handle.) Each child can make a list of the objects identified in a given time (perhaps two minutes). It will then be possible to compare lists and see who has the best sense of touch.

## Hearing

● Tape a collection of familiar sounds for the children to identify such as a doorbell, a telephone, the sound of a car engine or a motor cycle, a whistle, a pedestrian crossing 'beep', the song of a bird or the bark of a dog. You could include one or two more difficult ones such as someone cleaning their teeth or water being poured into a glass. If the sounds are numbered, it will be possible to do this as a quiz, with children writing down what they think each sound is as it is played back.

● Blindfold a child, then make a soft sound, perhaps tapping two coins together, in different positions near him or her. *Can you tell where the sound is coming from each time?*

## Sight

● Set up an eyesight test by sticking short familiar words in different-sized print onto a sheet of white card. You can cut these from magazines or newspapers or prepare them on a computer. Let the children test their own eyesight from different distances. This will show them how distance affects how well they can see and recognise features. *Is it better to use one eye or two? What difference does it make if you only look through one eye?*

## Taste

● Check first if any children have food allergies or if they might have religious or other objections to specific foodstuffs. Blindfold one child at a time and then, taking suitable hygienic precautions and keeping the child out of sight of the remainder of the class, let him or her taste and try to identify small pieces of strong-flavoured

food items such as apple, onion, chocolate, carrot, cheese, salt and sugar-free mints. Each child should be given a piece of paper so that they can later write down the foods they have identified.

● Explain the role of the tongue in the sense of taste. (There are four basic sensations of taste: sweet, bitter, sour and salt. All flavours are a combination of these four. See illustration below.) The test can be repeated with each child holding his or her nose to demonstrate the close relationship between taste and smell. *(Have you ever noticed how food has little taste when you have a bad cold and your nose is blocked up?)*

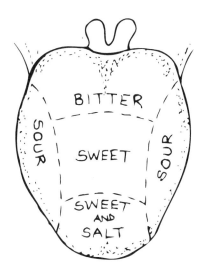

## Smell

Prepare a set of 'smelling' pots by putting five different materials with strong scents in each of five clean yoghurt pots. These could include flower petals, onion, cheese, chocolate, orange peel, coffee and paper towels or tissues soaked in vinegar or mint essence. Number each pot and cover it with muslin, pieces of tights, or foil perforated with a few small holes. Hold these covers in place with rubber bands.

● Pass one pot round at a time. Encourage the children to try to identify and write down what they smell in each pot.

● Let the children work in pairs or small groups to discuss which smells they like and which they dislike. Then discuss with the whole class how smells can help us to identify dangers such as smoke or gas. Take this opportunity to emphasise the dangers of smelling unknown substances in uncontrolled circumstances.

# Variation and classification

## Human variation

◉ Measure the heights of all the children in the class. *Who is the tallest?* Plot the results on a block graph. If there are not too many children in the class, separate graphs can be constructed for boys and girls. *Are the two graphs different? Which group has taller children?*

◉ If it is possible to do this without hurting the sensitivities of individual children, weigh everyone in the class or group. *Who is lightest? Who is heaviest?* Make a graph of the results.

◉ Measure the area of each child. One way to do this is for children to work in pairs. They take turns to lie down on a large sheet of squared paper while their partner draws around them. They then count the number of squares within the line, including all squares where half or more is inside the line. Alternatively, younger children might draw around each other's bodies (on newspaper or plain paper) and cut around the outline. Name the shapes and lay them on top of each other to see who in the class is the largest and who is the smallest. The shapes can then be coloured and displayed in order around the class with a heading suggested by the children.

◉ *Who has the largest hand?* Everyone draws around their left hand (with fingers together) and cuts out the shape. (Left-handed children can draw round their right hand.) *Whose hand is smallest?*

◉ Let the children suggest headings for a class

or group chart to record the characteristics of everyone's skin, hair and eyes. *Who has curly hair and whose is straight? Who has blue eyes and whose eyes are brown?*

◉ Compare fingerprints. Use an ink pad (the kind used for rubber stamps) which has washable ink on it. Roll the first finger of the right hand of each child gently on the pad. Then roll the inked finger on a piece of white drawing paper. (It may be necessary to practise several times to get clear fingerprints which are not smudged.) *Are any two of the fingerprints the same?* Explain that no two people have exactly the same fingerprints and discuss the use of fingerprints in crime detection. Destroy the fingerprint sheets at the end of the lesson, or allow the children to keep their own prints.

◉ Make a chart to compare the favourite foods, drinks, sports, colours, music, pets or television programmes of each child. *Does anyone have exactly the same list of favourites as anyone else?*

◉ Emphasise to the children that, unless they have an identical twin, there is no one else in the world who looks exactly like them. (Even identical twins have slightly different fingerprints.) No one else talks like them, thinks like them, or loves or hates exactly the same things. In other words, we are all unique.

## Grouping living things

◉ Allow the children to be 'wildlife detectives' in the school grounds or, with permission and extra adult supervision, in a local park. Working in pairs they should make lists of as many different things, both large and small, as they can find. Back in the classroom they can try to sort their lists into two categories: plants and animals.

◉ Suggest they try to sort their lists into further groups. They may need adult help to do this and they may find simple information and identification books useful. Animals can be sorted into groups such as 'Birds', 'Insects', 'Spiders' and so on, and plants into groups such as 'Grasses', 'Trees', 'Mosses' 'Ferns' and so on.

◉ Give the children a leaf from each of two different trees growing in or near the school grounds. *How many differences can you find* between the two leaves? In what ways are the trees themselves different? The children can enter their observations in a table with two columns.

⬤ Look for small invertebrate animals (minibeasts) around the school grounds or, with permission and extra adult supervision, in a park or some other public space. Search under stones, bark, pieces of wood, walls and hedges, reminding the children to set stones and pieces of wood back in their original position once their undersides have been examined. Encourage the children to examine the minibeasts carefully. *Do they all like living in the same place? How do they move about? How do they protect themselves? How do the animals see, smell and feel? How can we collect some of these animals without hurting them?* (A plastic spoon and a small paintbrush make ideal tools.) *Can you draw and name some of these creatures?* (They may have to invent their own names for some of the animals.) They could prepare lists of animals found in different places. *Which of the animals prefer dark, damp places?* (Woodlice are good ones to choose.) Let the children design and make a woodlouse home in an old shoe box, basing it on the knowledge they have gained.

⬤ Always remember to return the animals to their original homes after study.

⬤ With the children, make a collection of pictures of animals cut from magazines and old books. If possible, include examples of invertebrates (animals without an internal skeleton and backbone: insects, spiders, earthworms, slugs, snails, jellyfish, crabs, lobsters and so on) as well as members of the five groups of vertebrates. These are fish, amphibians (frogs, toads, newts and salamanders), reptiles (snakes, lizards, tortoises, turtles, crocodiles and so on), birds and mammals. *How many ways can you find of grouping the animals in the pictures?*

⬤ Collect five or six flowers from garden plants or weeds. *How many ways can you find of grouping the flowers other than by their colours?* Introduce the children to the names of the main parts of a flower to help them in their grouping. They might construct a simple table with two columns to compare two different flowers.
⬤ Make a visit to a zoo, wildlife park, wildfowl collection, bird garden, botanical garden or garden centre to give the children some idea of the huge variety of animals and plants in the world today. If this is not possible, make two big collages: one of plant and one of animal pictures. Start the collages on really large backing sheets so that you can continue to add pictures. *What shall we call our big pictures?*

## Materials and their properties
## Changing materials

⬤ Let the children see how we can change the shape of some materials by bending and twisting them. Use pipe-cleaners to make the bodies, arms and legs of some bendy figures. Attach small pieces of card, with faces drawn on, for heads. Make other figures, using plastic bottles, cardboard tubes or lolly sticks as bodies, and pipe-cleaners or small springs for arms, legs, and even necks. *How could you make springs of your own?* (Wrap a short length of wire neatly and evenly around a cylindrical object, such as a pencil, and then carefully remove the cylinder.)

⬤ Make a simple balance using a large rubber band. *What will happen if more and more beads or other small weights are put in the yoghurt pot?*

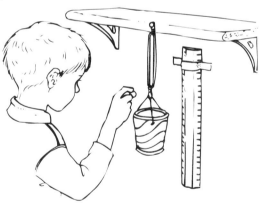

⬤ Find out how water changes when it is cooled. (This activity may need to be done with one small group of children at a time if space in the deep-freeze is limited.) Fill one or more balloons with water and tie the tops tightly. Put the balloons in carrier bags to avoid possible floods. The children can then (gently) feel the water-filled balloons. Put the balloons in a deep-freeze overnight. Let

the children (carefully) touch the ice balloons the next day. Peel the balloon from the ice and put the ice in a bowl of water. *Does it float or sink? Make observations about how the balloon changes shape as it warms up. Why is the balloon getting smaller? Where is the ice going? How could we find out?*

● Show the children some bread. *What happens if it is put in the freezer? What happens if we take it out again? How has the bread changed? Can we change it back? How does the bread change if it is toasted? Can we turn the toast back into bread?*

● Let the children test small quantities of substances to see whether they dissolve in water. Provide small, clear plastic containers and clean lolly sticks as stirrers. It may be useful to have hand-lenses available to help the children see whether the substances have really dissolved. Safe, soluble substances to use include salt, sugar, baking powder, instant coffee, bath salts and bicarbonate of soda. Safe, insoluble substances include pieces of crushed cork, vermiculite, flour, clean sand, sawdust, glass marbles, tea-leaves and crushed brick.

● Show the children that it is sometimes possible to separate dissolved substances from water. Dissolve some sugar or salt in water. (This can be done as a class demonstration or by the children working in pairs.)
Pour some of the solution into a clean saucer and leave it on a sunny windowsill, near a

radiator, or in a warm oven to allow the water to evaporate. The sugar or salt will be left behind. If conditions are hygienic, the children can taste the sugar or salt, although they should be warned not to taste other chemicals. They might have noticed the taste of salt on their skin after they have been swimming in the sea.

● The children can separate larger particles of insoluble substances, such as marbles or pieces of cork, from water with the aid of a fine sieve or gravy strainer. Smaller insoluble particles, such as those of sand and tea, can be strained off with a filter paper (or coffee filter) held in a funnel. Explain that a filter paper is really a kind of sieve with holes so minute that we can't see them. *What about a tea-bag? How do we know there must be tiny holes in it?*

● In small groups, the children might bake a cake or some currant buns. Discuss with them how, when we mix together the various ingredients such as flour, milk, eggs and currants, and heat them, we end up with a completely new substance – cake. Talk about other substances that are permanently changed by heating (eggs, meat, apples and so on).

● Prepare some dough by mixing flour and water into a thick paste. (If sufficient materials and facilities are available, children could do this in pairs.) Divide the dough up into three or four portions and bake each one in an oven for a different length of time. Discuss the differences in colour, texture, size and smell of the baked dough samples. Cut each one in half and compare their internal textures. If the conditions in which the dough samples were prepared were hygienic, the baked (unleavened) bread samples can be tasted. Compare samples of dough and bread made from different kinds of flour such as plain, self-raising, wholemeal or brown. Encourage the children to record the results of this activity by writing short sentences or producing drawings of the ingredients and finished products.

● Make some clay models and weigh them immediately. If possible, also measure the lengths of some of them. Weigh and measure the models again at daily intervals. *What changes have taken place? Why is this?* Record the results of this activity as a simple diary.

● Mix plaster of Paris with water until it forms a creamy mixture with the consistency of thick custard. (Children, working in pairs, might be able to do this themselves.) Pour some into a mould made from clay or Plasticine which has taken an impression from anything with a relief pattern on it such as large coins or medallions, the underside of evergreen leaves or LEGO bricks. Leave the plaster to set. Another interesting alternative is to leave a tray of smooth mud on the playground or playing field with breadcrumbs sprinkled around it. When a bird has walked in the mud, leaving a footprint, this can be surrounded by a small wall of card, filled with plaster of Paris and left to set.

Compare the consistency and texture of the solid and liquid plasters. Make a display of the labelled plaster casts.

● Use different types of squirters such as clean washing-up liquid bottles, syringes, water pistols and pumps to squirt water. *Does the water go further when we press gently or hard? How can we measure how far the water goes?* You will probably want to do this outside on a fine day!

## Physical processes

## Forces and motion

This is one of the areas of the Science National Curriculum which presents non-specialist teachers with some of their biggest worries, even though we use forces all the time. There are many types

and sizes of forces and between them they can:
● make a stationary object move;
● make a moving object slow down or speed up;
● make a moving object change direction;
● bend, twist or change the shape of something.

Quite simply a force is a push or pull or a twisting or turning movement. Some forces such as gravity, friction and magnetism are invisible. Other forces rely on contact. Some objects move because of forces applied externally. Others move because there is something inside them such as a clockwork or electric motor, which does the pushing or pulling.

## Push and pull

● Ask the children to push some toy cars along different surfaces, such as a smooth floor, a carpet and different textures of paper or cardboard. How can they ensure that they apply the same force to each vehicle on the different surfaces? *Which cars travel farthest? Which travel the shortest distances? Why is this?*

● Let the children take turns to handle a sponge ball. Discuss what happens to the ball when it is squeezed between the hands or stretched.

● Let the children work with clay or Plasticine to make a variety of shapes. Ask them to consider whether, when changing the shape of the clay or Plasticine, they are applying a push, a pull, or both to the material.

Use a pump to show the children that you can change the shape of a balloon by pushing air into it. The more air you push into the balloon, the more its shape changes.

Collect pictures of wheeled vehicles of all kinds. Ask the children to arrange the pictures in order of the size of the push or pull needed to move that vehicle. A large lorry, for example, would obviously require a much greater force than a roller-skate or skateboard. Point out that the push or pull for a big vehicle usually comes from an engine inside it, rather than from an external source. Display the ordered pictures with a caption devised by the children.

## Friction

Let the children investigate why moving things stop and introduce them to the rubbing force we call friction. They will probably appreciate that a sledge slides easily over snow because it is smooth (there is not much friction). However, the same sledge will not slide easily over rough grass (because there is lots of friction).

Ask the children to find small objects made of different materials such as a block of wood, a stone, an ice cube and a rubber. (Try to ensure that the objects chosen are roughly the same size and shape.) Prop up one end of a smooth piece of wood on books or bricks so that it forms a ramp. Hold the test objects in a line behind a ruler at the top of the ramp. At a given signal, lift the ruler quickly so that the objects can slide down the ramp. The first object to reach the bottom of the slope has the least friction. Record the results with drawings or short sentences.

Discuss which shoes offer the most friction. Examine the soles of trainers, sandals, wellington boots, and a variety of ordinary walking shoes. Can the children suggest ways of investigating which of two different shoes provides most friction? (One way would be to slide them down a ramp. The shoe which slides least has the most friction.)

Look at pictures of different kinds of tyres, including those of large earth-moving machines. The children may notice that machines which need to grip the ground, particularly in muddy or snowy conditions, have thick tread patterns.

*Is it easier to slide or roll an object?* Make a ramp from a smooth plank of wood propped on some books or a brick. Fill a round biscuit/cake tin with sand or toy bricks. Let the tin slide down the ramp on its base and then allow it to roll down on its side. *When does it move most easily?* Investigate different toys and domestic appliances that have wheels or rollers.

Fill a large box with books or bricks so that it is hard to push along. Try pushing it across a carpet and on a smooth surface. Then try moving the box on rollers, made from strong cardboard tubes. *Is it easier to move the box by sliding or by rolling? Why is this?* (There is less area in contact between the rollers and the floor, and hence less friction than there is between the base of the box and the floor.)

## Turning forces

Children should be aware that we often use forces to turn things. Opening a door by turning

its handle or unscrewing the lid of a jar are two examples. *How many more examples of twisting or turning forces can you think of?*

## Magnetism

⬤ Investigate the forces exerted by a magnet. Let the children find out which objects are attracted to a magnet. They will soon discover that objects made of, or containing iron or steel, will be attracted. They will also realise that like poles of two magnets (that is two north poles or two south poles) repel each other ('push each other away'), while unlike poles (that is a north and south or south and north) attract each other ('pull towards each other').

Use a magnet, a wire paper-clip and some sheets of paper to find out through what thickness of paper the magnet can pull the paper-clip. *What other materials will the magnet pull or push through?* (Try wood, cardboard, glass or plastic.)

## Gravity

⬤ Introduce the children to the force of gravity, using this word if you think they are ready for it. Take them out on to the playing field or playground, well away from buildings and overhead cables. Ask them to throw rubber balls as high as they can. *Do you think you could throw the ball so high that it would never come down again?* Explain that this is impossible, because the balls are pulled back to Earth by the invisible force we call gravity.

⬤ Investigate how things fall to the ground. In the sixteenth century the Italian scientist and mathematician, Galileo, showed that all objects fall at the same rate. He dropped a small and a large cannon-ball from the Leaning Tower of Pisa and found that they hit the ground at the same time. Ask the children to test Galileo's ideas. Give them small and large balls, or a steel ball-bearing and a large pebble. (If the two objects are dropped together from exactly the same height onto a metal tray, it is easier to tell when they both reach the end of their fall.) It may be necessary to point out that a steel ball-bearing will fall at a different rate from a sheet of paper or a feather. This is because the paper or feather has a large surface area for its weight and is therefore slowed by the air much more than the ball-bearing.

## Floating and sinking

Things float because of an upward force. You can feel this upward force if you try to push a large empty plastic bottle fitted with a stopper, or a large hollow ball, under the water. The force is called 'upthrust'. The deeper into the water the object goes, the more water it pushes out of the way, and the greater the upthrust becomes. When the upthrust equals the weight of the object, the two forces cancel each other out and the object floats. If the object is completely under water and the upthrust is still not equal to its weight, the object sinks.

⬤ Begin the study of floating and sinking by collecting objects of approximately the same size but different weights. The children can test them by putting them in a bowl of water. *Which sink to the bottom?* Discuss whether it is the heavy or light objects which sink. *Why do some things float in water?* The children can record their results in the form of a simple table with two columns headed 'Float' and 'Sink'.

⬤ The children's understanding of floating and sinking can be extended if they are asked to roll a lump of Plasticine into a ball and put it in a bowl of water. The Plasticine sinks. Now tell them to dry the Plasticine, roll it out into a thin sheet and mould it into the shape of a boat. The Plasticine now has a much wider shape for the water to push up. Although the weight of the Plasticine has not changed, it floats because it now takes up more room.

⬤ Things with air inside them generally float well, because air is lighter than water. The children will have seen that if you push down on a ball floating in water, the water seems to push back because of upthrust. You can take this a stage further by comparing the upthrust on three or four different-sized hollow balls, or three or four different-sized empty plastic bottles, fitted with stoppers, when they are pushed down into a container of water. In each case the children can be asked to note how great the upthrust is exerted by each ball or bottle. They should also notice what happens to the level of the water in the container as the object is immersed.

⬤ Float a metal can in a bowl or bucket of water. Add marbles or small pebbles, one at a time.

What happens to the can? What happens to the level of the water in the bowl or bucket? Why is this? Why does the can eventually sink?

Finally, in connection with floating and sinking, children often ask why a small block of steel sinks while a huge steel ship floats. The answer is again, the shape of the object. A small block of steel sinks because it is heavy for its size. By contrast, a huge steel ship has lots of air inside and is light for its size.

##  Ideas bank

### Humans as organisms

● Tell the children that they are going to play a chasing game to see what exercise does to their bodies. Ask them to predict what might happen. After they have been playing for a time, ask them about any changes they have noticed in their bodies (they may feel warmer, they may be sweating, breathing faster and their hearts could be beating faster). Discuss why it is important to take exercise even though it can make us feel hot and out of breath. Let the children draw pictures of themselves before and after exercise for a display.

● Give the children mirrors (ideally plastic ones) and talk about their reflections. What shape is your face? What colour are your eyes? What colour is your hair? Is your hair long or short? Is it curly or straight? Do you have freckles? Let the children draw self-portraits based on their observations. Ask the children to draw their faces showing different moods – they could be happy, sad, angry, afraid or surprised. Display all these drawings.

● Make a large display of pictures showing the different stages in the growth and development of human beings.

● How far away can a watch be for its ticking to be heard in a quiet room? Test each ear separately. Does one ear hear better than the other? Compare children with adults and make a simple chart of the results.

● Working in pairs, ask the children to blindfold one partner who must then pinch his or her nose. Taking suitable hygienic precautions, the blindfolded child should then be fed tiny cubes of apple or onion by the 'seeing partner'. Can you always tell these foods apart by taste alone?

● Make a collection of pictures and photographs, or models of objects which use pattern and/or colour to make them easy to identify or to give information (perhaps a police car, a fire engine, an ambulance, a post-box, traffic lights, a zebra crossing and various commercial logos). Discuss which colour is used most often. Which colours are not used at all? Why are some colours used more often than others?

### Variation and classification

● Collect information on the shoe sizes of all the members of the class. Plot those of boys and girls separately on simple block graphs (or prepare a simple database beforehand). How many people have the same shoe size? Do boys have bigger feet than girls?

● Compare the muscle strengths of members of the class. Use bathroom scales and see who can produce the highest reading by squeezing the scales with both hands. Who can press hardest with one finger?

● Compare the size of the children's hands. Who can hold the most cubes in their hand? Who has the longest hand? Who has the widest hand span?

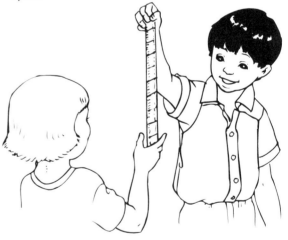

● Working in pairs, one child should dangle a metric ruler, so that its bottom end is midway between the partner's separated thumb and forefinger.

At a given signal, the ruler is let go and the partner tries to catch it as quickly as possible. How far does the ruler fall before it is stopped? (The point at which the ruler is caught gives an indication of 'reaction time'.) *Who has the quickest reactions?*

## Changing materials

● Seal a large ice-cube inside a plastic bag and weigh it. Let the ice melt. *Will the water weigh more or less than the ice?*

● Experiment with sugar lumps to see how many can be dissolved in a jar of cold water. Try very warm water. *Can you dissolve more sugar? Does it dissolve more quickly?*

● Year 1 children often confuse dissolving with melting. Let a wax candle melt and drip into cold water. *What happens? Does the wax dissolve?*

● Working in pairs, children can investigate changes in food substances by making some chocolate crunchies. (Adequate supervision should be available to ensure safe and hygienic working practices.)

Melt fifteen cubes of chocolate (plain chocolate is best) in a heat-proof bowl by standing it in a larger bowl of hot (not boiling) water. Add two cupfuls of puffed rice cereal and mix thoroughly.

Spoon the mixture into paper cases or a non-stick bun tin and allow the mixture to cool and harden. The recipe makes approximately sixteen cakes.

Let the children taste the ingredients as well as the final cakes and compare the colour, taste and texture. *Can we change the chocolate crunchies back to the materials we started with?*

## Forces and motion

● Give the children a collection of different materials such as felt, sandpaper, carpet or plastic floor covering. Working in groups, can they devise a test to see which materials have least friction and which have most friction?

Supply blocks of wood, string, sticky tape, strong rubber bands, drawing pins, hooks, small plastic buckets and non-standard weights (such as marbles). Be prepared to supply other equipment (within reason). The standard test (see illustration) is to wrap each piece of material in turn around a block of wood, fixing it with drawing pins. A hook is then put in the end of the block and the block is placed in a marked position on a table-top.

Finally, a bucket is attached to the hook with string so that it hangs over the edge of the table. The friction can be measured by the number of weights that have to be placed in the bucket to

move the block along the table-top.

Help the children to work out this method for themselves, though you should also be receptive to children who devise other methods. One group fixed the pieces of material in turn to the soles of one child's shoes with rubber bands and pulled him along the floor by his arms – judging the friction of the different materials by how hard it was to pull him along.

● Go on a visit to a playground or fairground (or examine pictures of them). Find examples of pulling, pushing and twisting forces. Discuss them, then let the children draw one example of each kind of force.

● Float a polystyrene ceiling tile in a bowl of water. Load it with washers or toy bricks until it sinks. Alternatively, use unperforated plastic bags or plastic bottles to make an object which normally sinks such as a marble, ball-bearing or stone, float.

● Let the children take turns to feel the upward push (upthrust) acting on a large hollow ball that is forced underwater. Allow the children to let go suddenly so that they are able to observe the

springy force exerted by the water. (This activity is best carried out on the playground.)

● Put a rubber band around a transparent container of water to mark the water level. Let the children observe how the level of water rises (water is displaced) when various objects are pushed under the water.

● Make a collection of rolling and non-rolling items such as boxes, cans, plastic jars, pencils and solid shapes from the maths cupboard. *Ask: Can you predict which shapes will roll?* Let the children test their predictions and then examine how the objects roll (for example in a straight line or a curve).

● With rollers such as cricket stumps, old broom handles or thick cardboard tubes, let a small group of children try moving a classmate along the floor on an upturned table. *Can you organise yourselves into a team to transfer the rollers from the back to the front?*

● Make a collection of wheels. *Can you tell where these wheels came from? In what ways are they different? Why?*

# Assessment

By the time you have finished the work with your Year 1 class, you will have a good idea as to whether the children enjoyed the topics and which style of teaching was most effective. You should also be able to judge how much the children have learned by evaluating each topic against the criteria with which you started.

## What do they know?

There is no set list of facts they should know, but all the children should have gained something, although that something will vary from child to child. By the end of Year 1 you might expect most of your class to know:

- the names of the external parts of the body, expressed verbally, with labels or with clear symbols (Sc2);
- that humans need food and water in order to stay alive (Sc2);
- that our senses help us to know what is going on around us (Sc2);
- that humans have babies (Sc2);
- that there are many different kinds of plants and animals (Sc2);
- how to sort the different groups of plants and animals from their shape and appearance (Sc2);
- that there are lots of different materials (Sc3);
- that materials change when they get hotter or colder or when they are shaped (Sc3);
- whether things are going fast or slow and which way they will go (Sc4);
- the difference between a push and a pull (Sc4);
- that some objects float and some sink (Sc4).

## What can they do?

They should be able to:
- describe objects and materials (Sc1);
- describe things that happen (Sc1);
- talk about what they saw (Sc1);
- make a record on a table consisting of two columns (Sc1);
- draw what they see (Sc1);

Science

## What have they experienced?

They should have:
- examined a variety of living things;
- handled a variety of materials;
- carried out simple experiments under guidance;
- experienced a variety of pushes and pulls and other forces.

## How have they made their knowledge public?

Pupils should have discussed their work with others and displayed their findings through drawings, simple models, graphs and tables and, where possible, by means of short sentences written with the help of the teacher.

# History

History is an essential part of the 'broad and balanced curriculum' you must offer your Year 1 class and you should continue to draw on the National Curriculum programme of study - which is not an intimidating one – it can be fitted on to one A4 page, and is summarised in two sentences.

Pupils should be given opportunities to develop an awareness of the past and of the ways in which it was different from the present. They should be helped to set their study of the past in a chronological framework and to understand some of the ways in which we find out about the past.
*History in the National Curriculum,* DFE, HMSO, 1995.

The programme of study is divided into two main parts: areas of study (content) and key elements (skills and ideas).

The two are, of course, inter-linked, but are best developed through the areas of study.

**Everyday life**
* Everyday life in the past (from the familiar to the more distant in time and place).
* Changes in the lives of the children themselves, their family or adults around them.
* What it was like in Britain at some point beyond living memory.

**Famous people**
* Famous men and women (including some from British history).

**Past events of different types**
* Past events of different kinds (including some from British history).

The first problem is to sort out which areas you will cover in Year 1. Some content overlap (and indeed repetition) in Year 2 is acceptable but the programme of study should be properly allocated or an inefficient curriculum free-for-all will result.

School policy may dictate which content is allocated to your class but the context in which Year 1 children will study the past is likely to be a general topic, the kind that usually begins with the children and their own experiences, and it is best that this comes first and is taught to Year 1. This social history can easily be linked to teaching about everyday life in the past. Past events, particularly notable anniversaries and commemorations (the Coronation, harvest or the Gunpowder Plot) may be discussed at any time during the infant stage. Most schools choose to leave a specific history project and finding out about famous people until Year 2.

The kind of topics that work well with Year 1 children are:
* grandparents (or substitute, such as the lollipop lady);
* me and my family (a chronology of growing up);
* teacher as a child;
* holidays (now and then);
* toys;
* harvest;

● the story of our railway station (or some other well-known local building, such as a house, a school, or a shop).

However you choose to package your history, it should link with the world that the child knows. Even the world of television and video provides some sort of experiential link. Always keep Year 1 history simple and direct, as well as highly visual and tactile (meet grandma, visit the station, play with the Edwardian toys, etc).

# What should they be able to do?

If children are given appropriate tasks, it is surprising just how much history they can cope with in Year 1. But very young children will not spend as much school time on history as older children, so aims and expectations should therefore be few and reasonable. Historical skills and knowledge are acquired slowly so reinforcement and repetition are necessary throughout the key stage.

The following is a guide to suitable expectations of the average Year 1 child in relation to the subject's key elements. These five key elements include the skills and ideas essential to the subject that will be taught through the content. You are not expected to teach each key element every time you teach history but you do need to ensure that they will be covered gradually over the key stage.

## Key element : Chronology

Clearly the young child's ability to cope with time is very limited, and clearly too, when you are struggling with single digit numbers, dealing with tens of thousands is out of the question, thus the use of dates is inappropriate.

But five- and six-year-olds can gradually learn to distinguish past time from present time, they can come to know that the past existed and that it is different from the present. Generally they can understand too that the past was big.

The ability to grasp even these simple notions is closely associated with language skills, especially the use of correct tenses and the ability to employ a reasonable vocabulary of time. Errors will still occur (*I am having a party yesterday*) but they will be diminishing.

A surprising amount of adult/childhood talk is time related. *What's the time Mr Wolf?, Once upon a time, Bedtime!* When they are used regularly these phrases begin to acquire meaning, and so the child's vocabulary of time-descriptive words is gradually extended (*bedtime; playtime; yesterday; now; before; after; today; tomorrow; the days of the week* and so on). Year 1 children will not always use this vocabulary with unerring accuracy any more than they will count faultlessly. At this stage telling the time is in its infancy.

You cannot expect Year 1 children to use dates to order things sequentially, but they will be able to place two objects or events in time order if these are within their experience and on a large enough time scale. A child at Level 1 will happily sort dinosaurs and cars into time order (oldest to newest) and, with practice, deal with more subtle differences between objects or pictures (tell an old iron from a new one). Arranging three objects in time order is more challenging. Children can cope with this kind of sequencing when it is carried out as a concrete operation, but not when it is primarily a verbal or intellectual exercise, although when the past is in story form they tend to find it more manageable.

Year 1 children should be able to re-tell a simple story, placing the main events in the correct order. Most children can distinguish events that happened when they were babies from nowadays.

# Key element: Range and depth of historical knowledge and understanding

In Year 1, children are at a kind of 'pre' history stage, rather like the early stages of learning to read or coping with number when basic concepts and subject ground rules are being established. Put aside all thoughts of teaching any kind of political or recognisable academic history. The clauses of the 1832 Reform Bill and Tudor foreign policy are not the sort of history young children can understand or 'know' in any meaningful sense.

Children of this age gain their knowledge and understanding of the past through stories; through talking to people about their own pasts; and through contact with objects. By these routes they begin to establish a number of stereotypical images of, for example, a 'king', or a 'Roman' or 'Victorians' although their grasp of these terms is very different from that of adults. As Year 1 children first become aware of the past as a vague amorphous mass, their early understanding will tend to take a simple cut-and-dried form, full of sharp demarcations between 'goodies' and 'baddies'.

By the end of Year 1, most children will be able to talk about their own past (*My first word was 'tractor'*.) and have acquired some information about other 'pasts' (*At my mum's school they used to have desks with lids that opened*.). Their awareness that 'then' and 'now' are different has begun to grow. Most Year 1 children are at a stage where they are working out boundaries and beginning to draw distinctions, such as learning what is theirs and what is not theirs - a process that also applies to their experience of history. They are developing the ability to apply labels to situations and objects and establishing definitions.

A good measure of the historical understanding of Year 1 children is the extent to which they ask questions about the past and are themselves beginning to give simple answers to similar questions.

## Key element: Interpretations of history

The past is presented to us and interpreted in many different ways; through pictures in books, museum displays, television programmes and so on. As Year 1 children are only just beginning to distinguish between past and present, they will not readily cope with distinctions between different representations of the past. However, they should have an expanding vocabulary that will assist them in making these distinctions at a later date (they should, for example, know what a film is).

Most children of this age will also recognise different versions or interpretations of familiar stories (for example 'Goldilocks and the Four Bears' – there are many published versions of this sort) and, through practice, can develop this habit of perception and prepare the ground for later historical work. (*How is this story different from what we know?*)

## Key element: Historical enquiry

This key element focuses on how we find out about the past, ultimately it is about evaluating evidence and sources.

Year 1 children should understand that we can find out about the past by asking people who have been alive for a long time. By the end of Year 1 they should have had experience of interrogating people about their pasts (oral evidence) and realise that this is a way of getting useful information – although at this stage they will be developing the skill of asking questions rather than questioning answers.

Infants learn best from hands-on direct experience and the closest they can come to this in history is to handle evidence. Direct experience of the past is obviously impossible but wearing a helmet once worn by a Roundhead, or using an iron that great granny used to use, is the next best thing. Five-year-olds should be able to recognise many objects that are 'old' and be beginning to understand that we can learn about the past from them. (Don't forget that a castle or a house is an historical object in just the same way as a hay cart or a quill pen.) This kind of understanding will, of course, only develop if children are given a great deal of experience of handling evidence and are encouraged to ask questions about it and think about its origins.

For obvious reasons, most documentary sources are inaccessible to children of this age, although they might handle (in play perhaps) and appreciate the function of an identity card from the 1940s or an old advertisement.

If it is not possible to handle objects, Year 1 children cope well with pictures – which are the next best thing. They will already recognise a photograph as a special form of picture. By looking at pictures they will be able to distinguish an old car from a modern one and will begin to appreciate that we can tell what it was like in the past by looking at old photographs.

## Key element: Organisation and communication

Most children of this age are very limited in their ability to communicate, although it is probably their most rapidly developing skill. As has been said before, Year 1 children's grasp of history will be closely related to their language skill and whether they can speak clearly, organise their thoughts coherently and have an adequate vocabulary to talk about the past.

Talk will be the main medium for communicating and most Year 1 children will be able to describe a few events in sequence or re-tell a simple story. Information gained from talking to an older person about his or her childhood will be recounted in the form of simple statements and single sentences. Longer narratives will be less common.

Another means of communicating knowledge, again predominantly verbal, is that of creative play and teachers who observe children at play will see them acting out being a Victorian scullery maid or being at grandma's school. You can help children to communicate in this way by providing them with a range of creative play opportunities through the use of props, such as a Victorian stove in the home corner.

A few children will be able to make public their historical knowledge through drawings or simple written sentences.

## Planning for history

History is not a major component of the Year 1 curriculum but it still has to be planned for, otherwise it tends to get missed out.

Plan for:

● **on-going history** – learning opportunities that are present all the time such as artefacts on the 'tinkering table'; story and picture books in the book corner; words and labels on displays (names of the months of the year, for example);

● occasional **class topics** with a history content – almost certainly general topics, such as Myself or My School, but with a planned history element;

● **serendipitous history** – look for useful opportunities for historical learning (perhaps if a child brings an old photograph to school).

Most of the preparation for on-going history can be done before the term starts.

● Collect a few appropriate objects for the children to handle, discuss or sort. These can be used selectively throughout the year. If the school or your own private resources are inadequate, check with the local museum service which may well have objects available for loan. Car boot sales are often good cheap sources for useful objects such as old hand whisks, irons, clothes pegs, books or toys and, of course, parents and members of staff will often be able and willing to lend artefacts.

● Prepare flash cards or labels for display and for the word bank.

● Make sure that you have suitable story and picture books to read to the children and to put in the book corner for them to look at themselves. (There are lots of splendid books with stories about grandma and grandpa and there are many others with useful historical content such as *Wilfred Gordon McDonald Partridge* Mem Fox (Puffin), which explores the meaning of the word 'memory'.)

● Collect pictures. Next to objects these are the most useful teaching aids for infants. The school may have photographs of its own early history or that of the local community. All of these will be useful. What pictures you need will depend on the topics you study and the objects you display in the classroom but there are now many excellent commercially-produced collections for schools. Educational magazines such as Infant Projects, Child Education and Junior Education (Scholastic) are another useful source.

Plan when your history topics are going to take place. You may want to avoid mixing history topics with Christmas or Harvest celebrations (unless that is part of your planning!). If you are bringing in outsiders to talk to the children, you will need time to organise these visits. The personally-related history topics are fine for early in the year, although you will need to know the children, and their families, reasonably well to make sure you do not intrude into sensitive areas.

Opportunities for teaching history that arise serendipitously cannot, by their nature, be planned for. All that is required is that you are quick to spot these opportunities and are able to judge which to take and which to reject. It is just as bad to miss all the opportunities as it is to squeeze history out of every possible opening.

## Allocating time

You may never teach a precisely measured quantity of history at this, or perhaps any other level, in the primary school, but you should aim for a target range of time within which your teaching should fall. You are likely to refer to this figure only when you are undertaking your long-term planning.

A target time of 36 hours in a school year, or 3% to 4% of curriculum time, is reasonable at Key Stage 1 although, depending on the kind of topics that you choose, you might do considerably more. If in any one term you are undertaking a topic with a main history focus, such as 'Me and my family', then you might allocate 24 hours in that term but only 12 hours in another term. It is not sensible to try to allocate the hours on a week-by-week basis, but to consider the longer term .

This time target is a planning and reporting aid. Auditing with accountancy precision is not required.

# Practical ideas

## Making a start

Invariably teaching begins with a 'concrete' experience (handling an object; visiting a museum) or a story. Next comes talk. Children need to learn to observe and to question. History, with young children, virtually begins and ends with *What? How? Why? When? Where? Who?*

## Developing key areas

### Ordering pictures

● Pictures with a Velcro backing can be easily moved and manipulated. Ask the children to place familiar pictures on a wall-mounted calendar strip. This can be a very simple seasons calendar (summer, winter, spring, autumn) on which the children have to place correctly holiday photographs, Christmas pictures, Harvest pictures and so on. This calendar can become a semi-permanent time-chart.

● Why not organise a visit by the time fairy? First, imitate a fairy. She (or he, if you wish) mischievously takes down the carefully arranged pictures overnight. *Who can put them back correctly?* When the children have got used to this game (don't play it with too many objects at once) let the time fairy move just one picture. Can the children spot the change that this despicable creature has made?

### Stories

● Tell a simple historical story and select groups or individuals to act out parts of the story as you re-tell it. This could be a story such as the Gunpowder Plot, although an anecdote describing an incident when you were at school could be just as effective.

● After telling an appropriate story, provide suitable props for play in the home corner. (Florence Nightingale tending the wounded; a child playing with a spinning top; a servant cleaning shoes with boot polish; doing the washing using a 'dolly'.)

● Either individually, or as a class exercise, ask the children to sequence pictures illustrating the main events of a story that you have told. Use storyboard pictures (the children might make their own).

## Pictures and objects

● Use a series of objects to show change over time. These could be simple domestic items such as writing implements, lights or hot water bottles. Discuss the age of these and get the children to place them in time order.

● Pictures or objects can be left on the tinkering table for children to arrange in time order (oldest – newest – the one in the middle).

● Match actual artefacts with pictures of the same objects being used. (perhaps a carpet beater with an old photograph of a maid using one.)

● A variation on the above is to start with people (in picture form or perhaps you or a visitor acting out the role) and select the objects (or pictures of objects) that the character might have used.

● Obtain a class photograph from the 1950s and a current one. Give the children pictures of school equipment (or preferably the artefacts themselves) to sort into two groups to match the children in the photographs. You will have to decide on what is most suitable for your particular class, but you could try old/new desks, uniform/jeans, satchel/plastic lunchbox, computer/old textbook, wooden bricks/LEGO or plastic construction kits.

Collect together pictures of families from two distinct historical periods (perhaps today/1950s or turn of the 19th century/turn of the 20th century). You might even be able to draw your own pictures. The children could use these to play simple matching games (objects to families or domestic events to families). Sets of family cards can be made for games of Happy Families or Snap. By playing these games children will establish stereotypical images of particular times in the past and learn to identify period clothes and objects.

## Visitors

Invite a suitable elderly person to come into school so that the children can ask questions about life in the past. Prepare the children by discussing appropriate questions. It is worth arranging a return visit, possibly with a photograph album to browse through. Use your imagination to make the most of a visit like this. Can you make a link with a child in the class? Is there an opportunity to share experiences of different backgrounds, origins and cultures?

## Children's own history

Make a picture album to tell the story of each child. Most children will love sharing photographs of themselves as babies with the rest of the class. Make sure you keep the parents informed on this one, as they need to understand what you are doing. Not every childhood is conventionally straightforward and some children may not have baby photos.

Construct zigzag timelines showing the main events in each child's life - when they were born, when they first crawled, their first step or word,

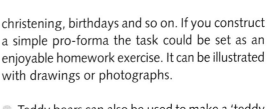

christening, birthdays and so on. If you construct a simple pro-forma the task could be set as an enjoyable homework exercise. It can be illustrated with drawings or photographs.

Teddy bears can also be used to make a 'teddy bear timeline' on a similar basis to the last suggestion. Use your own old teddy if you have one. Alternatively, make big displays around your chosen teddy showing the world when teddy was 'born'. There are a number of variations on this theme. Be creative!

## Acting the past

Turn the creative play corner into a simple social history experience with opportunities for acting out the past as it was in the 1960s or 1950s. (You can go further back in time but props will not be quite so easy to come by.) Borrow appropriate items and clothes for dressing up from parents. Make a 1950s front room (you could try making a replica TV) or create a 1960s wardrobe. You may be able to find an old telephone, photocopy a 1950s comic, borrow old toys and domestic appliances. The set-up does not need to be too complex. Link the corner with a story, pictures or a visit.

## Visits

Investigate the possibility of a visit to a museum or site, such as a mill-worker's cottage, that links with the social history that you are teaching. With children of this age you must be careful to restrict the focus of the visit and not travel too far. It would be impossible to include a comprehensive list here, but some good examples include: 19th century railworker's cottage, Swindon; 1950s living room and TV programmes, Museum of Film and Photography, Bradford; 1940s pre-fab, Avoncroft Museum of Historic Buildings, Bromsgrove; Victorian School, Sevington, Chippenham.

## Resources

Most commercially-produced wallcharts and educational picture collections are too complex to use with children of this age. However some infant history schemes include collections of suitable visual resources.

Photographs are an excellent source, particularly those which show people in situations the children will recognise (weddings, at the seaside, family groups). A picture of a former headmaster, vicar or blacksmith can be a good starting point for talk. Photos of people engaged in domestic activities are also useful (watching an early television, turning a wringer, cooking). Photographs with a clear single focus (a seaside pier, railway station, a school) and of places that the children know (the High Street, the school, the town hall) are especially useful for comparisons of then and now.

Of course a photograph of an object does not quite match up to the real thing, but you cannot always produce an old bus, a steam train, a sailing ship or a castle for the children to examine! Pictures of unobtainable domestic objects are useful for the same reason as they can be handled and examined at will.

It is probably best to steer clear of photographs of reconstructions, if only because there are plenty of real pictures available so there is no need to use them at this stage.

Contemporary paintings are invaluable if you are dealing with a period beyond the era of the photograph. Victorian paintings can provide a useful counter-weight to the dominant black and white photographic images children come to associate with the past.

## Sources to explore

● Old photograph albums.

● School archives (check what old pictures lie buried in the stock cupboard).

● Local museums and libraries. (The children's librarian should be able to help. In the adult section look out for coffee-table books of old photographs of your county or locality.)

● National museums (the National Portrait Gallery perhaps, or local stately homes).

● Museums of childhood (there are quite a number now but those at Bethnal Green, and on the Royal Mile in Edinburgh, are the most famous).

● Old postcards (try The Frith Collection, Andover, Hampshire SP10 5AR for pictures of your locality).

● Birthday, Christmas and nostalgic picture cards – even the wrapping paper used in some shops can be a useful source.

## Suitable objects

You may need to buy very little to build up a school collection of suitable artefacts. First ask colleagues and parents. Try jumble sales, car boot sales, the attic, the back of the stock cupboard (again!) and charity shops.

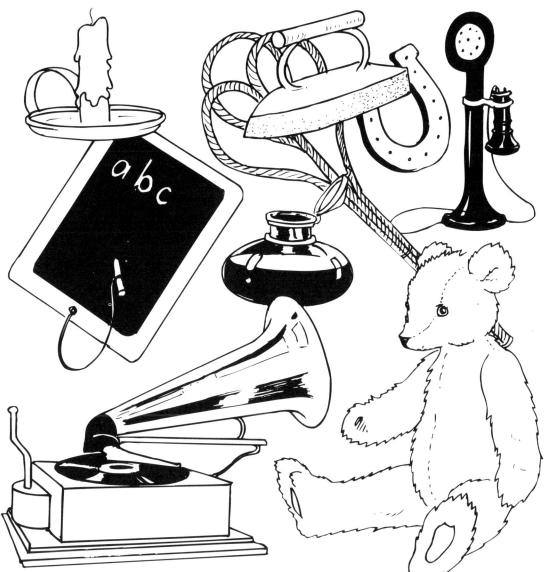

Borrow from anyone who will lend (check on the school insurance cover). Most areas have active County Museum and Library services which operate loan systems.

Reproductions from specialist suppliers are rarely a cheap option but you might like to consider History in Evidence (mail order, Chesterfield), Past Times (mail order, Witney, and retail shops in major cities). Museums, too, can provide reproduction objects and these are not always very expensive, for example Victorian smocks from Armley Mill Museum in Leeds.

The kind of things that you should especially watch out for are:

● everyday objects which illustrate change in the domestic world (horseshoes, scrubbing brushes, clothes horses, carpet beaters, flat irons, button hooks, knife cleaners, glove stretchers, wind-up gramophones or leather suitcases);

● collections which can be used for sequencing or to show development (rush light – candle – light bulb or early wireless – transistor radio – personal stereo);

● objects with a school connection (slates, sand trays, inkwells, old books);

● childhood objects (toys, clothes, books, nursery items such as rattles, christening robes and so on);

● adult objects (clothes, shoes, uniforms).

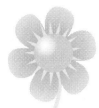

# Assessment

Children in Year 1 have barely begun to comprehend what history is so, when it comes to assessment, very rough measures must apply.

If you need a written assessment of a child's performance in history then it is best to assess against a few very simple performance indicators. These should relate either to teaching targets you have set yourself or to the kind of attainments identified in the Level 1 and Level 2 descriptions.

These include:

- good understanding;
- partial understanding;
- no understanding;
- knows that the past exists;
- knows that it is different from the present;
- understands simple everyday words (*before/after/long ago*).

# Geography

During Key Stage 1 the children will be learning about small localities, starting with their local area. This will be the immediate vicinity of the school, including the school buildings, the grounds and surrounding area within easy access, probably within walking distance for the children. They will compare this with contrasting localities of a similar size. They can learn about another locality in, for example, your city, a nearby village, a neighbouring town, or in 'natural' countryside. You may prefer to choose an overseas locality with which you are familiar.

Key Stage 1 children are also likely to be learning about aspects of the world about them, such as the quality of the environment, the weather, or jobs and journeys.

There are four key areas of geography in which your children should be progressing:

- ability to undertake geographical enquiry and use geographical skills;
- knowledge and understanding of places;
- knowledge and understanding of geographical patterns and processes;
- knowledge and understanding of environmental relationships and issues.

These are fundamental to geography.

In Year 1 you will be developing the children from their introduction in reception. The emphasis will continue to be on providing spatial experiences in school and in its immediate environment, extending children's language both for describing their environment and for talking about their experiences, and improving and extending their ability to use and make maps and pictures.

In their immediate environment (whether natural or manufactured) the children should be given opportunities to:

- explore and work out routes from first-hand experience;
- use all their senses to develop wonder, curiosity, respect for people, cultures and places;
- share responsibility for this environment, becoming aware that their actions and those of others can improve or spoil it;
- make, record, question and communicate their observations, and make comparisons;
- develop and test ideas through observation, discussion and reflection;
- develop a sense of self and their place in home and school communities, by talking about themselves, family, friends and events.

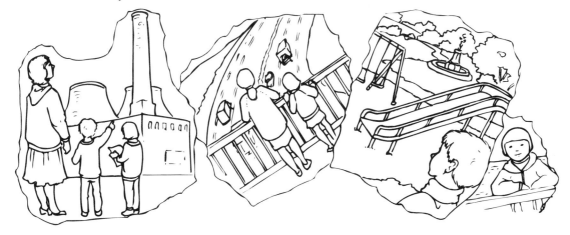

The children should also explore similarities and differences between their own immediate natural and/or manufactured environment and others with contrasting physical and/or human features. They can carry out an extended study of one contrasting locality, but you should aim to broaden their experience by introducing a range of localities, possibly in less depth, for example in *hot and cold, wet and dry, near and far, north and south, natural and manufactured (built) places*. Choose places with which you are familiar, with which the children in your class have connections or which are in the news.

# What should they be able to do?

In Year 1 you should provide, either in designated geography lessons or in topic or thematic work in which the geography is explicitly identified, activities in which the following four key areas of geography are integrated.

## Key area: Geographical enquiry and skills

They should develop and extend their ability to:
● understand and use geographical vocabulary;
● respond to questions about places and environment topics on the basis of information you have given them;
● make, record and communicate their own observations about places and environment from first-hand experience and secondary sources such as photographs, books, videos and CD-ROMs;
● carry out simple enquiries by undertaking fieldwork tasks and classroom activities using and making maps, diagrams, photographs and other resources you provide.

## Key area: Places: features and comparisons

Most children should be able to recognise, express views about, describe and begin to record:
● the main physical (*landscape, weather*) and human (*buildings, routeways*) features of their local area, and any other localities they study, using appropriate geographical vocabulary;
● that places change (*the effects of weather, new buildings or roads, a shop that changes its function*);

● that buildings and land are used for a variety of purposes (*living, playing, learning, working, travelling, recreation*);

● the significance of location, why features are where they are, why things happen where they do (*the location of local pedestrian crossings or CCTV cameras, where the grass gets worn off the football pitch, where new building or demolition work is taking place*);

● similarities and differences between the places they visit and study, comparing and contrasting localities.

## Key area: Patterns and processes

They should respond at varying levels to questions about:

● where things are, the location of important buildings or services (*the shops are in the middle of the village/town/estate, the fire station is in Cornwall Road*);

● physical (natural) and human processes, including trying to explain why things are like they are (*why part of the classroom/school is in the shade in the morning but in the sun in the afternoon, why buses go along some roads but not others*);

● the pattern of how things change (*day or night changes including human activity, light, temperature, relative position of the sun and moon; weather changes or patterns; traffic changes or patterns such as rush hour or the weekend; water level in a stream*).

## Key area: Environmental relationships and issues

They should:

● express their own views about physical and/or human features of their environment, recognising attractive and unattractive aspects (*I like my garden in summer when there are flowers in it, because . . .*);

● recognise that their environment changes and that people affect it (*the street's messy outside the take-away when people drop the plastic boxes*);

● appreciate that the quality of the environment can be improved (*the playground would be tidier if we put our crisp packets in the litter bins; the street would be better if people didn't let their dogs dirty the pavement*).

These aspects are looked at in more detail in the Practical ideas section on page 98, although the focus is on geographical skills and enquiry, the real tools of geography.

# Practical ideas

## Making a start

### Where are you?

In PE (in the school hall and in the playground) play a version of 'Simon says...', inviting the children to stand *in* a hoop, *on* the mat or bench, *next* to or *against* the wall; to place a bean bag *under* their foot, *above* their head, *behind* their back, *in front of* their face, and so on. Introduce distance and direction.

### Make judgements

Encourage the children to make quality or aesthetic value judgements and to express an opinion about individual aspects of their own environment, about the classroom, pictures, videos, school grounds, use of materials (for clothing, building, toys and so on). Help them to realise that they will not all have the same opinion and encourage them to justify or explain their likes and dislikes. Reinforce their opinions by placing 'smiley' and other faces in the appropriate places.

## Developing key areas

### Geographical vocabulary

Give your children opportunities to learn geographical language and special terminology through direct experience, practical activities and fieldwork, from TV, pictures, stories, role play and games. (In Year 1, early geography will often evolve from play, especially for children who have not been in a reception class.)

● Continue to develop and use the everyday language of:

▶ direction (*right/left, up/down, forwards/ backwards, straight on, round the corner, over/ across, north/east/south/west*);

▶ location (*here/there, near/far, next to, behind, in front of, above/below, on/under*);

▶ form (or shape), scale and distance (*big/small, bigger/smaller, long/short, longer/shorter, straight/curved, close/far away, closer/further*

away, nearer/farther, high/low*, and, of slopes, *steep/gentle*). They should also be able to express distance in *steps/paces/metres/kilometres*;

▶ quality and aesthetics (*quiet/noisy, pretty/ ugly, tidy/untidy, clean/dirty*; also comparatives *quieter, tidier* and superlatives *quietest, tidiest*;

● Use this language whenever opportunities arise: in PE, in the classroom, walking around the school, the school grounds and the neighbourhood. (Much of this vocabulary is relevant to the mathematics curriculum, too.);

● Continue to make geographical vocabulary lists – some words will be universal (such as weather) but others will be specific to your school, your local area and your chosen contrasting locality, including the features which give these places their particular character.

### I-Spy

● Use walks, visits or pictures to introduce and practise the names and characteristics (colour, size, shape, materials, function and so on) of:

▶ features in the natural or physical environment, including landscape, water in the environment and weather, building on the vocabulary learned in the reception class;

▶ features in the built or human environment, including settlement, economic activities, jobs, journeys and transport.

## Role play

Encourage the children to act out geographical contexts associated with shopping, industry, agriculture, transport or holidays. For example Act out all the stages of going on holiday – booking (travel agent), packing (all members of family), travelling (passengers and providers), holidaying, returning, telling (from different characters' perspectives) – using appropriate geographical vocabulary).

## Walks

Make full use of opportunities to go for short walks around school, the school grounds, the neighbourhood and further afield to develop children's skills of:

**Observation:** Identify landmarks and routes, take photographs of landmarks (houses, shops, street furniture, open spaces), distinguish between fixed (buildings) and moving (people, traffic) features;

**Memory and recall:** can they remember, and recognise, photographs of what they saw? Draw pictures of landmarks or sort photographs into piles of 'saw/didn't see';

**Sequencing:** Can they sequence photographs of landmarks into the correct order? Can they sort them into 'seen on right/seen on left' or 'seen on High Street/seen on London Road'?;

**Description:** Acquire and use geographical vocabulary to label or describe landmarks, describe the route taken in words, in drawings or in large maps.

## Literacy Hour

Reinforce geographical language development by devoting a regular part of Literacy Hour to geographical words and stories. (This is not geography unless you explore spatial, geographical aspects of the stories, but it does practise the vocabulary.)

# Geographical knowledge

Continue to develop the children's geographical general knowledge.

● Create opportunities to talk about places the children have visited, where their relatives live, that they have seen on TV, or encountered in stories.

● Add to their knowledge of local, national, global places and features (*towns, villages, cities; areas of countryside; countries; seas and oceans;*

*rivers; mountains*) reinforcing with pictures if possible. Locate the places and features on maps and globes – full conceptual understanding will come later.

# Geographical enquiry

Throughout your work you will be posing geographical questions about places, about parts of the school, its grounds and neighbourhood, about a visit, a story, a picture, a TV programme, for the children to respond to. In addition, you will also be encouraging them to ask and seek answers to their own geographical questions. You will be beginning to extend their geographical thinking beyond 'observe and describe'. Through the questions you pose you will be encouraging them to categorise or classify, to compare, to conjecture, hypothesise and speculate, to express opinions, and to consider values and attitudes.

# Local place study with a question framework

Questions should form the framework for a Place study, in particular your study of the immediate locality of the school (see box on page 100). You will be introducing the children to the idea that to some questions there is no one right answer, that there may be a range of responses, none 'better' than others, because people have different opinions. (Later they will learn about consensus and decision-making.)

Take your children on a field visit or geographical walks in the area immediately around the school. As you carry out fieldwork ask:

If there is something they didn't like: *Can we do anything about it? Whose responsibility is it?*

Back in the classroom, use the children's drawings or photographs for recall, description, sorting, sequencing and locating the visited area on a large-scale map.

Encourage them to make their own representation of the locality, perhaps a pictorial map or pictures, and talk about them, using their newly-acquired vocabulary.

A local study of this type will be an extended geographical project. You could use a similar framework for the contrasting locality, visiting it if possible, otherwise relying on the use of photographs and video material.

## Interrogate photographs

Use photographs to ask different types of question. Even the youngest children will be able to handle the six types of question identified on page 101. They should be asked throughout the primary school – progression will be achieved through the challenge or complexity of the question and its context. So, when working with a photograph of a market in India (a distant locality), you could ask:

## Quality of environment study

The classroom is a good environment in which to carry out a practical 'quality of the environment' study, providing opportunities to 'observe, question and record, and to communicate ideas and information'.

What do you like and dislike about it, find attractive or unattractive? Why?

| What is it? | Observe the physical and human features of the locality and give them appropriate name-labels. Make drawings or take photographs to use later in the classroom. |
| --- | --- |
| What is it like? | Describe the human and physical features of the locality, using the appropriate name-labels. Record what you see: draw, take photographs or use a camcorder. Express an opinion about the locality and its features; the feel, appearance, condition, size, colour, aesthetics and so on. |
| What sort of place is it? | Categorise the buildings, the place and its features. |
| Is it like any other places you know? | Compare it with other places with which the children are familiar. |
| Where is it? | Communicate its location in different ways – verbally (using distance, direction and locational language with reference to school, using its official name, address, even post code); using a large-scale map; making a model and/or a picture map; finding it on an aerial photograph. |
| Why is it like it is? | Encourage conjecture about this. |
| How can/will/did we get there? | Describe the journey and route from and back to the classroom, locate it and colour it in on a large-scale map – this will help the children to see the shape, length and direction of the route relative to school. Again encourage the use of language of direction, location, distance and so on. |
| What do you feel about it? Do you like it? | Encourage the children to express, explain and compare their opinions, values and attitudes. |

| Concrete | What can you see? |
|---|---|
| Descriptive | What are the people doing? |
| Speculative | Why are some of the things spread on the ground? |
| Reasoning | Why do some people have umbrellas when it isn't raining? |
| Evaluative | Is there a good choice of fruit and vegetables? |
| Problem Solving | The traffic is all mixed up with the market. What could be done about that? |

What makes a part of the classroom 'nice' or 'nasty', pleasing or unpleasant, or even warm or cold?

How can the classroom environment be improved? Who should do this?

Can the improvement be maintained?

Introduce ideas of individual and collective responsibility. You might also like to introduce the collection and recording of data by:

- dividing the class into areas or zones, recording these on a big plan;
- giving each area daily or weekly scores for being, among other things, tidy, clean or colourful. These scores could be represented pictorially;
- using the scores mentioned above for number work – are they increasing or decreasing, is the area improving or deteriorating?

## Real issues

This study (outlined in the box on page 100) could be developed further to allow you to study another part of the school, the school grounds or the neighbourhood. There might be a real issue in school that the children could tackle – the storage and tidiness of games or PE equipment perhaps, or use of the playground for different playtime activities.

If a real issue about the quality of a local environment is featured in the local newspaper, use this as a focus for a study. Suitable issues might include proposals to pedestrianise the local shopping centre, problems with a pond in a local park or closing (or building) a leisure complex or business park in the area.

## Graphicacy skills

Graphicacy, 'the essentially pictorial communication of spatial information', has been described as 'the fourth ace in the pack', alongside literacy, oracy (articulacy) and numeracy. Geographers think it is possibly as important, as a life skill, to be graphicate as to be literate, articulate and numerate.

## Spatial information

Year 1 children should continue to develop and use their graphicacy skills for:

- acquiring spatial information, including way-finding, understanding signs and symbols, using pictures, photographs, diagrams, aerial photographs, maps, plans, globes and atlases;

- giving spatial information, including making pictures and diagrams, making maps and plans.

## Way-finding

- Go for walks to find routes around the school, the school grounds, and the local area/ neighbourhood. Recall them afterwards in the classroom, through talk, drawing and map-making.

- Play **Where am I?** Name a starting point that is familiar to the children, describe a walk from this point, encouraging the children to visualise where you are as you describe your route, stop, then ask *Where am I?* You might, for example, start at the classroom door and stop your route in the school hall.

## Pictures, photographs, videos

● Continue to build up a comprehensive collection of photographs of the school, the school grounds and the local area, in all weathers, in all seasons, and at different times of the day. (It is very useful – and considerably cheaper – to have multiple sets of prints made at the time of processing.) If you have access to a video camera, you can add video tapes to the collection. These can be invaluable for many activities.

● Describe, match, sequence, and locate on a large model or plan.

● Name, describe, remember, recall, sequence, ask *What's next to...? What's opposite...?* and so on.

## Using different perspectives

● Take photographs of the school and its locality from unusual perspectives; match them to photographs of the same features taken from ground level; talk about where the features are in relation to the classroom and where the unusual views are taken from.

● Take three photographs (side, oblique and vertical view) of different children; sort them into sets – same perspective, same child.

● Identify and label features on an aerial photograph of the school.

● Compare the aerial photograph of the school with a large-scale plan.

## Maps, plans, globes, atlases

● Use pvc floor maps (you can write on these with washable felt-tip pens) to locate places the children know, or those with family connections.

● Play ball with inflatable globes; recognise land and sea; introduce names of continents and oceans; compare with a rigid, mounted globe, orientating similarly.

● Have a range of picture, road and world atlases available in the book corner.

## Diagrams, models and plans

● Use diagrams, especially 2-D representations of 3-D structures, to make models and constructions from, for example, LEGO or Meccano.

● Paint boxes to create the rooms of your school and label them appropriately. Use the boxes to model the school, placing the rooms on an outline plan of the school (painted on an old sheet for easy storage). Encourage children to identify features on the model, then record the model in pictures and plans.

● Play *What is it?* as an introduction to plan view. Encourage the children to recognise the shape or form of familiar objects from less familiar perspectives by placing small toys and other objects on the OHP and projecting the image. Laying the object on its side gives the familiar view, but standing it up gives a plan view. *Can you draw the views?*

## Maps from play

Provide play opportunities for the children to make maps. Their early attempts will be very simple and they will need repeated opportunities to develop their graphicacy skills.

● Use the train set: ask the children to draw round their track lay-out to record it and make a map (1:1 scale) then ask another child to reconstruct the lay-out from the 1:1 plan. Children might record their lay-outs in picture, and then in map form. Provide increasingly complex lay-out plans, or photographs of lay-outs, for the children to construct. Take photographs of a few lay-outs from different

perspectives (side, oblique and vertical view) for the children to sort by perspective or lay-out.

⬤ Use the sand tray: provide a range of different materials, either separately or mixed together (such as builders' aggregate, dried peas, rice, beach sand and pebbles, 'grow-bag' compost and so on). The children create landscapes – a hill, a mountain, an island - and add features such as hedges, trees, roads and LEGO buildings. Record their landscape in picture and then in map form. *What happens when it rains (watering can) on the mountain? What happens when you try to create the sea round an island? Can you make cliffs, caves? Can you make a river or a lake?*

⬤ Use LEGO: a group of children could make buildings, group them to make a settlement, use sugar paper and crayon (or chalk) to make a village or town lay-out or their own 'play mat' (a 'map' showing houses, gardens, school, shops, parks, roads, paths and so on). Add more buildings. *Is the town or village the same all through the year? Where do the people live? How do they move around? Where do they go?* Introduce ideas about weather, seasons, jobs and journeys, economic activity. Make a map from the lay-out or 'play mat'.

## Geography from stories

Develop geography from stories by asking geographical questions. Encourage children to imagine the spatial relationships within the story, and to represent them as pictorial maps. Introduce the children to distant localities through story.

## Weather

⬤ Talk about the weather daily to use and expand the children's weather vocabulary. Start recording with informal measures (recording temperature, sun, wind direction and strength, rain, cloud) to keep a weekly chart. Encourage

the children to invent symbols to draw the weather. At the end of each week; compare the chart with the one for the previous week. Transfer the data to the computer.

⬤ Observe the following things and ask the children to explain why:
⬤ different parts of the classroom and playground are sunny at different times of day;
⬤ some parts of the playground are windy and some sheltered;
⬤ playground litter gets blown in different directions at different times, but usually collects in the same places;
⬤ puddles usually occur in the same places.
Record the observations on a model or large plan of the school.

Link these observations to questions: *Where do you most like to play, and why? Where would be a good place to put a new big flower tub or a new playground seat, and why? What happens to the rain?*

⬤ Observe and record where the rain that falls on the school buildings and grounds goes to. It is fundamental that children appreciate that water flows downhill – watch it on a steeply-sloping roof and gently-inclined playground. *What happens on concrete or tarmac, on grass or ground that has been dug up? Do puddles form on all these surfaces? Why/why not?*

Watch flowing water move dirt, gravel, fallen leaves. Watch small channels form. Watch water flowing off a sloping bank or playing field edge, transporting mud and then depositing it.

All this will help the children to create images and form an understanding that later on will give them a clearer perspective on the formation of streams and rivers and, eventually, of a river system.

## Information technology

⬤ Introduce children to *My World*: both 'Weather' and 'Make a Town' are suitable geographical programs.

⬤ Use a concept keyboard with geographical overlays: enlarged photographs of the school's locality; of distant places; an aerial photograph, and a simple map of the school grounds for the children to label, enter simple captions and write about.

# Assessment

In Year 1 you will want to keep a simple record of the progress children are making:

## What do they know?

Particularly in terms of geographical vocabulary used appropriately to label, describe and tell about places and their physical and human features.

## What can they do?

Way-finding, use of geographical skills, ability to ask and respond to geographical questions, find information, give opinions, make comparisons.

## What have they experienced?

Resources, topics, activities, fieldwork (experiences outside the classroom).

## How have they demonstrated their knowledge?

Evidence through talk, drawing, map-making and using, writing, practical activity (sorting, matching, sequencing).

# Music

In this year you should be drawing together many threads, consolidating ideas already explored and discovering new things together. In doing this you will be leading towards the National Curriculum suggestions that, at the end of Key Stage 1, that children should:

- sing a variety of songs and play simple pieces;
- explore, select and order sounds;
- make some use of the musical elements in simple compositions; these elements should include dynamics and timbre;
- respond to short pieces of music – they should listen attentively and begin to use simple musical terms.

At all levels, music should be seen as an important part of the whole school curriculum, to be integrated with other subjects but also to have an identity of its own.

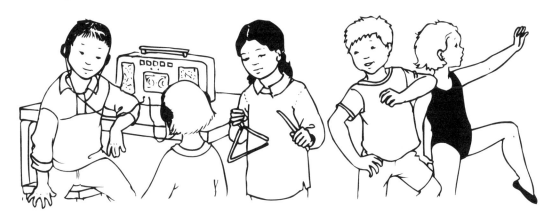

## Key areas: Listening, composing, performing, appraising

A curriculum for music making will always ask for sounds to be explored through listening, composing, performing and appraising and, at times, it can be useful to look at these areas separately. However, in any successful music session all four are in action at the same time. Music makers, whatever their age and experience, listen to sounds, collect them, discuss them, choose appropriate ones and place them in a structured way, move them around until they are satisfied and then perform them. This is no less true for children in Year 1 than it is for students of music at a University and should be encouraged at all times. All these skills will be used in the activities suggested in this chapter.

The activities explore all the elements of music as suggested in the National Curriculum. These are:

- Pitch (high/low);
- Duration (long/short);
- Dynamics (loud/quiet/silence);
- Tempo (fast/slow);
- Timbre (tinkling/rattling/smooth/ringing sounds);
- Texture (one sound or more sounds);
- Structure (building a piece of music).

A music session, although usually very enjoyable, can sometimes lack purpose, as in: *Let's have a sing song; Shall we play on the instruments?; Now dance to this music.* If you are aware of the musical elements, and direct a session towards their exploration, the work becomes more focused, interesting and appropriate.

# What should they be able to do?

## Key element: Pitch

Pitch refers to high and low sounds. Children do not find it easy to understand the concept of a high sound and a low sound and really have to experiment in order to learn. They will point to a high place and a low place but, when asked to sing a high note or a low note, will have difficulty doing so. Many children find this confusing and mix up the two sounds. At this early stage of music making, children need to listen carefully to many high sounds and to many low sounds and to notice that there is a difference in how they are created. Their explanation might be as simple as: *You sing a high note out of the top of your head and a low one deep in your throat* or *A high note on the xylophone/ chime bars/ glockenspiel is made on the shorter bars and a low one is made on the longer bars.*

The most important activity for music-making children, however, is listening. Some may have been actively encouraged to listen for specific sounds by parents or in the reception class but many will still find it quite hard to listen for a particular (high or low) sound. After some encouragement they should find it both challenging and fun. It would be hard to listen to high and low sounds without hearing that sometimes a sound slides from high to low, or vice versa. This can be the source of much exploration.

By the end of Year 1, most children should recognise high sounds as distinct from low sounds and be able to create them vocally. They should have some understanding of how a high or low sound is made, both vocally and on an instrument, and they should be using these sounds in simple pieces (repeated high sounds contrasting with repeated low sounds).

## Key element: Duration

Duration in music means the length, or brevity, of a pulse, a beat or a rhythm. All children will have had experience of making long and short sounds from a very early age and should have no problem understanding this concept. At this stage, your aim should be to encourage them to control their long and short sounds so that they become more regular, more organised, in fact more musical. Joining the long and the short sounds together in a pattern gives us a rhythm. During Year 1, most children will be capable of listening for long or short

sounds in the environment and should be able to identify the difference. They should be listening to the differences in sounds made by a variety of things (aircraft, birds, diggers, wind, rain) and deciding whether the sounds made are long or short.

They should be able to sing long and short sounds, controlling some long notes by taking long breaths as well as creating very short vocal sounds. When they are using their own bodies as instruments (body percussion) children will find that they can only make shorter sounds and should be encouraged to think about why this is. (Because the body has no resonance.)

Instrumental experimentation will show that some instruments are much better for making long sounds than short sounds (cymbals/glockenspiel/gong/chime bars) and that some instruments simply cannot make a long sound (wood blocks).

By the end of Year 1, all children should have experimented vocally, with body percussion and on instruments, to make and have some control over, long and short sounds.

## Key element: Dynamics

Dynamics in music refers to the difference between loud, quiet, silence, and getting louder or softer. All children are used to making loud sounds, but being quiet and observing silence is quite difficult for them. We live in a noisy world, where children hear many loud sounds as background noises without identifying them, so soft sounds often get lost. We need to teach children to listen to, and then explore, both loud and soft sounds. These sounds can then be collected on tape for use at a later date.

Sounds which get louder or softer can also be identified (cars driving past the school, footsteps walking down the corridor, aircraft overhead). The voice can make effective loud and soft sounds and is therefore a good instrument to use when controlling sounds that change from soft to loud. Body percussion also lends itself to exploring dynamics, since you can clap, click, stamp and hand clap softly and loudly, and move easily from one to the other. Any available instruments should be used to find out how loud and soft, controlled sounds can best be made. Encourage the children to explore and discuss how holding the beaters in different ways and exerting different amounts of pressure can vary the sounds.

By the end of Year 1, most children should have a good understanding and control of soft (*p*), loud (*f*), getting louder (*crescendo*) and getting softer (*diminuendo*) and should recognise the need for some silences in music.

## Key element: Tempo

Tempo, at this stage, means fast and slow. Children will already understand that some sounds can be fast and others slow, so your aim in music making will be to help them to make a specific slow sound or controlled fast sound.

Sounds that are out of control are generally not very musical. The voice can be used to sing fast sounds and, with practice, to sing longer sounds to achieve specific effects (tongue twisters, lullabies). Body percussion can be used to explore fast and slow rhythms - making a marching action with the feet is particularly effective. Instruments, including any made by the children from scrap items such as tins, squeezy bottles or wood, can be made to play fast or slow. By the end of the year, the majority of children should be in control of the pace at which they are asked to play in any medium (voice, taped sounds, instruments, body percussion) and should be able to move easily from a calm, regular sound to a slower or faster sound.

# Key element: Timbre

The quality of a sound that makes it different from every other sound, is called its timbre. Most children will begin the year by thinking that all sounds are similar, though some will be recognised as loud and soft, or short and long. They will need to listen very carefully with you to hear that each sound has something about it that makes it different from another sound.

Voices are a good starting point in the discovery of timbre. By listening to each others' voices at the beginning of the year, children will hear that each voice is recognisable, but different. The sounds that can be made by using the body as an instrument (clap, click, stamp, slap) are also quite different from each other and making up combinations of these (clap, clap, click, stamp) will accentuate these differences.

Every type of instrument, whether it is a chime bar or a bassoon, has a very special sound and your aim should be to present the children with different timbres so that they will begin to distinguish between them.

At this stage, the children should recognise the differences between instruments that have tinkling or rattling, smooth or ringing sounds and should be able to group instruments according to their timbre.

By the end of the year, most children should recognise the differing sounds of voices and instruments and be using them to create a variety of effects.

# Key element: Texture

The texture of music refers to the combination of sounds being sung or played together (even if this is just one sound played or sung on its own). It is like comparing a piece of material woven in wool (one voice) with another woven in wool, silk, and cotton (voice, guitar and castanets).

Key Stage 1 children may not understand the subtleties of the texture in music but will certainly enjoy putting a variety of sounds together and should recognise that some are more effective than others (very loud drums do not mix well with quiet singing voices, but bells and triangles together give a pleasant effect).

By the end of the year, pupils should have had plenty of opportunities to put sounds together and discuss the combinations which work best.

# Key element: Structure

All the elements of music – pitch, duration, dynamics, tempo, timbre and texture – should be thoroughly explored by the children in the course of Key Stage 1. These can be treated as independent elements, but much more interesting music will be created if a structure is introduced.

Just as single words are used to build a sentence, and the sentences need to be placed in a structure (beginning, middle and end) to make a story, so to create a whole piece of music, sounds need to be placed in simple structures, making use of the elements (pitch, dynamics, and so on).

Consider creating pieces with names such as 'Soft, Loud, Soft Music' or ' Let's Repeat Ourselves'. Most pupils need a great deal of help to master the use of simple structure (beginning/middle/end or repetition) but their eventual achievements will show that this is time well spent.

# Practical ideas

The best way to involve a whole class in musical activities is to make sure that you can see all the children and that they all have an unobstructed view of you. Sit them in a circle whenever possible, insist on silence while you give your instructions and make sure you have eye contact with them all. Activities should be very short and should change frequently - try alternating a listening activity with a movement activity whenever possible.

## Making a start

### Listening

● Open the windows and listen to the many different sounds in the environment. Ask the children to help you make a list of them.

● Open the window, but this time ask the children to listen only for sounds that are high or low. On other occasions, listen only for sounds that are loud and soft or short and long. Collect some of these sounds on tape to be used in music making at a later date.

● Listen in silence to the sounds in the school. Can the children hear footsteps coming nearer (getting louder) or going away (getting softer)? What else can they hear? Are the sounds loud or soft, long or short, high or low? Discuss them. Listen again, are there any new sounds?

● Take the children on a listening walk. Choose one specific type of sound to listen for. This could be getting louder or softer sounds, loud, soft, high, low, short or long sounds, even sliding sounds.

● With the children, sit in a circle. Ask them to copy you as you make a variety of sounds. *Can you sing these high notes?... Now try these low notes...I can make my voice sound very quiet, can you?... Listen as I slide down these notes. Can you do it?*

● Now, starting yourself, try to pass one single sound around the circle. Change the sound when it comes back to you again. This will take some

practice, so limit the time you spend on the activity initially. Try again another day with a different sound. Once the idea is established, let the children start and change the sounds.

## Introducing new elements

### Using the voice

● Move your hand up and down slowly and ask the children to watch and listen carefully as you sing high and low notes which follow the movement of your hand. Keep this very simple to begin with. Then ask the children to sing along, still following your hand movements.

● Draw a wavy line on the board or a sheet of paper. Point to the line as you sing the highs and lows. Can the children do the same? Ask one child to come and point to the line while the other children sing. Explain to them that in doing this they are acting as conductor.

● Use your voice to make the sound of a train, plane, helicopter, bus or tractor. Ask the children to copy you but agree first (and have a practice) on a hand signal for silence.

Once the sound has been established, show how this can get louder or softer as the vehicle moves nearer to you or further away. Ask the children to copy you. You may find that using a hand signal (opening or closing your hand) will help to control the sound.

● Help the children's diction in singing by listening to songs requiring careful pronunciation such as 'Supercalifragilisticexpialidocious' from *Mary Poppins* and 'The Court of King Caractacus' (Rolf Harris). Ask the children to sing along with the recording.

Pass a long sound around a circle using voices or instruments (perhaps small cymbals or chime bars). Let the sound ring until it has completely disappeared before passing it on. Then pass a short sound round the circle. This will take much less time.

## Listening together

Sometimes it is a good idea to just sit and listen to a piece of music, without asking the children to respond in song, dance or movement. Make sure the music is ready, that the excerpts are short and that there is a purpose for the listening. *Hands up when you hear a very loud sound. Hands up when you think the music is getting softer. Can you hear that the music is being played again? Listen again.*

Short sections of *The Sorcerer's Apprentice* by Dukas would be suitable for this *Can you hear the music of the magician? Do you think it really sounds like magician music? Why?... Listen to the water swirling into the room... Tell me when you think the spell is being cast by the apprentice.*

'Little train' by Villa-Lobos shows sounds changing as they come nearer and 'Bolero' by Ravel offers good opportunities to listen for crescendo.

## Body percussion

Pass a short clap around a circle. Pass two short claps, then three. Ask the children to copy you as you start the pattern. Keep it very simple or the children will lose the flow of the sounds and it will not feel controlled. Try the same activity with knee slaps and finger clicks.

Make flash cards (see illustration). Decide with the children which one best represents a clap, a click, a stamp or a slap. Ask them to respond as you show them the flash cards.

Place the flash cards in a line. Can the children read them from left to right, (as when reading a piece of music) and can they play the agreed sounds as you point to the cards?

## Using instruments

Play 'Copy me' with the children, using as wide a variety of instruments as possible, with the main intention of showing the class how to hold the instruments and the beaters. Explain and demonstrate that a much better, clearer sound is produced when the instruments are held correctly. This could be a good time to emphasise that instruments are not toys and will only play well if

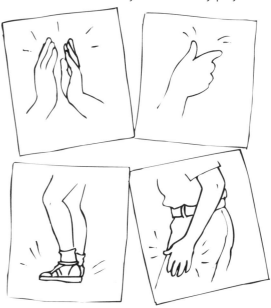

they are properly looked after. (Beaters need to be safely stored in a box or tin, untuned percussion should be carefully placed in a large box or on a percussion trolley, and tuned percussion should always be put away complete with all notes in the correct places. Labelled positions for each type of instrument in the storage place will provide additional reading practice.)

Provide as many different-sounding untuned percussion instruments as possible (triangles, tambourine, castanets, drums, wood blocks, and so on). Then sort the instruments by sounds (rattling, tinkling, shaking), discussing how each one makes a different sound. *Can any of them make more than one kind of sound?* Hand out the instruments, and ask the children to find all the people with an instrument that sounds like theirs (noisy, but fun). They should then sit down in a group and put their instruments on the floor. Explain that you are the conductor, and that when you point to a group you would like all its members to play until you stop pointing at them, or point to another group. You might like to introduce this by working initially with one child from each group, then two, then more. Move quickly from one group to another. *Make sure you are silent when another group is playing.*

● Select three instruments, one to blow (recorder), one to pluck (guitar) and one to shake (maracas). Play each individually. Ask the children to talk about each one. *Which do you like the most and why? Do you understand how the different sounds are made?* (Wind, vibrations, rattling rice.) *Can you think of any other wind, string or shaken instruments?*

● Use a tuned percussion instrument, preferably a xylophone (wooden bars), a glockenspiel (small metal bars) or a metallophone (thicker metal bars). Hold the instrument for everyone to see with the narrower end at the top and the wider end at the bottom. Take a beater and play from top to bottom. *What do you hear?* (They should be able to recognise the high sounds from the shorter bars and the low sounds from the longer bars.) Turn the instrument around so that the wider end is now at the top. *What happens now?* This should help them to recognise that high and low sounds are related to the length, rather than the position, of the bars. Show the children that the instrument is usually played with the long, low bars on the left, and the short, high bars on the right.

● Put up a screen and place a box containing a variety of different-sounding instruments behind it. Choose one child to go behind the screen and play an instrument for the others to hear. *Which instrument sounds like that?* Give several children a chance to be players.

● Ask three children to go behind the screen. (Stand where you can see the children behind the screen as well as the rest of the class.) Let each child choose an instrument. All three should play together, then indicate to one child to stop

playing. *Who can hear which sound is no longer there?*

● Play a game based on 'Simon says'. *Simon says play the tambourine, Simon says play the triangles. Now play the drums.* (Mime playing the instruments.)

● Encourage the children to experiment with the instruments to make new, unusual sounds, for instance, sliding a beater along a xylophone, covering the sound hole of a chime bar with a small piece of card.

## Writing it down

Place a large sheet of paper on the floor, in the centre of a circle of children. Have colourful crayons handy and six different-sounding instruments. Shake a tambourine once. *Can anyone draw a picture of how that sound might look?* It might be a squiggle like a worm or a high to low squiggle. The children will probably come up with a number of ideas, but try to agree on why one might be better than another. Play a wood block and draw a new sound. Usually there will be similarities in the symbols and these can be discussed. This is the beginning of graphic notation and can be very useful for children who create their own pieces of music at this early stage and would like to record them.

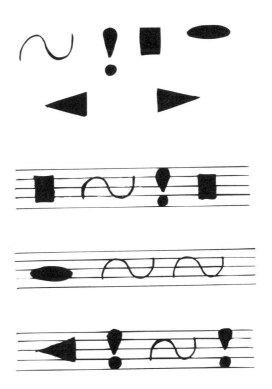

# Developing key elements

## Encourage everyone to sing

Sing with the children at every opportunity. If you are confident, then let the children copy you as you sing new songs. If you feel happier with help, find good recordings of appropriate songs and use them often. The Early Learning Centre stock some excellent tapes for young children, and the Singing Kettle group in Scotland have produced entertaining tapes of their songs. Your local library may have tapes which you can borrow – this is a good way to check on which tapes you like enough to buy.

Try to link songs with your projects. Repetition is the key to success at this stage and action songs help the memory. Always encourage shy singers to join in – consider asking a best friend or a more confident singer to sit next to them for support. Discourage shouters or very loud singers by asking them to listen to others and then join in. Sing tongue twisters to encourage clearer diction.

● Sing well-known songs or rhymes. Then ask the children to miss out one of the lines, singing it in their minds (internalising) and see if everyone can arrive together at the beginning of the next line.

● Learn a new song by singing it line by line, asking the children to copy you. If you are not a confident singer, use a recording of the song and

all copy the tape together. Stop and start frequently. Sometimes a child will already know the tune, or pick it up quickly, and could be asked to help in teaching the song. It is very important that everyone should be encouraged to sing – so involve anyone who is available to help. Young children are much less critical of singing voices than we sometimes think.

● Keep the songs short and simple so that the children can memorise them easily. Actions to songs make them enjoyable and more memorable. Look for songs that ask for body percussion movements ('If You're Happy and You Know It', 'First You Make Your Fingers Click' (*Flying a Round,* A&C Black), 'My Hands Upon my Head I Place' (*Gently into Music,* Mary York, Longman)).

## The sound of voices

● Listen to the sound of each person's voice. *Are there any two voices that sound the same?* The children should quickly realise that each voice has a sound of its own and can therefore be recognised.

● Agree on a phrase that should be spoken. 'Who am I?' might be appropriate. Ask all the children to close their eyes, then touch someone on the shoulder to speak the phrase. Can the children recognise who it is from the sound of the voice?

● Repeat the voice game but this time ask the children to try to disguise their voices so that they sound like someone else: a policeman, the lollipop lady, granny, granddad or a teacher. *Can anyone guess which child is speaking now?*

● As you tell stories to the children, use your voice as an instrument whenever possible. Use high sounds for women's voices and small animals, use low sounds for men's voices and large animals. Sometimes use the wrong kind of sound to see if any of the children notice what you have done.

## Name games

● Use name games as a means of introducing the children in your class to each other. Ask each child in turn to say his or her first name to the class, then follow this pattern: *Say your name. I'll clap it, you clap it, we'll all clap it.* Once the

children have the idea of the name game, they should be able to keep a steady beat running through the pattern. *Amy* (child), clap clap (teacher), clap clap (child), clap clap (all). *Jack* (child), clap (teacher), clap (child), clap (all).

Try singing the register with the children. Give them two notes to use (such as soh me, in tonic solfa or G, E on the piano or xylophone) and ask them to sing their own name back to you in turn.

Fit as many children's names as possible to the tune of 'She'll Be Coming Round the Mountain':

> *There's Alice, Chloe, Kim Pan in our class,*
> *And there's Manjit, Holly, Hannah in our class.*
> *There's Sarah, Geeta, Andrew,*
> *Ravi, Mark and William,*
> *There's Sadiq, Megan, Isla in our class.*

## Body percussion

Using the body as an instrument is great fun, so encourage the children to use these convenient instruments as much as possible. Hand clap, finger click, foot stamp, knee slap whenever it is appropriate. Look for songs that include these actions and make up songs of your own to the tunes of well-known nursery rhymes and TV. jingles. A&C Black's book *Bobby Shaftoe Clap Your Hands* by Sue Nicolls has many useful suggestions.

To the tune of 'Heads and Shoulders' try to move to:

> Clap and click and slap and stamp,
> slap and stamp,
> Clap and click and slap and stamp,
> slap and stamp,
> Nod your head and turn around,
> Clap and click and slap and stamp,
> slap and stamp.
> Begin by singing this quite slowly -
> the tempo will soon quicken.

## Music for stories

Read a story that will lend itself to sound effects. Well-known stories such as 'Jack and the Beanstalk' or 'The Gingerbread Man' make good starting points. Discuss with the children which instruments could be played for the cow, footsteps (Jack's and the Giant's), the beanstalk growing (low to high), climbing (moving in steps), wind, Jack chopping down the beanstalk, the beanstalk falling (high to low), and so on. Choose the instruments carefully and give them to a few children. (A small group of players will be more effective than a whole class of instrumentalists.) Read the story again with the sound effects.

*We're Going on a Bear Hunt* by Helen Oxenbury, and *Skyfire* by Frank Ash, both lend themselves to musical interpretations. *Bright Ideas for Music* (Scholastic) also gives some good ideas for child-created stories.

## Music to dance to

Young children have wonderful imaginations and will readily create movement stories to the sounds of recorded music. Play Elgar's 'Giants and Fairies' from *The Wand of Youth* and ask the children to imagine what is happening in the music. Can they, in small groups, make a dance to show everyone the fairies and giants?

'The Dance of the Automatons' by Claus Wunderlich is also lovely music to move to.

To reinforce the sounds of high and low, play 'The Swan' from Saint Saen's *Carnival of the Animals*, inviting the children to move up and down to the music as it flows along.

Listen to 'Step in Time' from *Mary Poppins*. Ask the children to clap in time, click in time, then can they step in time?

● If you are a pianist or can play any other instrument, you will be able to use your instrument to introduce the children to the elements of pitch, duration, dynamics and tempo. Ask for a response in dance to the way you are playing. Make up stories to match your playing. Encourage anyone who has dancing lessons to give a demonstration to the class.

## Animal music

Talk to the children about farm animals. *Have you heard sheep calling their lambs?* Explain that each mother and baby has a sound that is special to them, the lamb always knows how to find its mother by the sound she makes. Divide the class into two groups. One group are to be sheep and to bleat low sounds, while the other group are to be lambs and bleat high sounds. Mix the two groups so that sheep and lambs are spread evenly around the room. After a moment of silence, ask them to start bleating. Each lamb must find a sheep and then sit down.

## Collecting sounds

Some children may have access to a tape recorder at home. Encourage these children to go on a listening walk with an adult to tape specific sounds (high, low, short, long, loud, soft). Ask them to bring the tape to school so that the whole class can listen and try to guess the sounds.

## My favourite instrument

Many children have a particular instrument they enjoy playing. Invite them to talk about their favourite instrument to the rest of the class. *Why do you like the sound? How many sounds can you make it play? How does it make you feel – happy or sad? Who else likes the same instrument? Are your reasons the same or different?* Invite each child to demonstrate their favourite instrument to the class.

## Making instruments

Many schools have difficulties in providing enough instruments for all children to play. One good answer to this is to make a few of your own. Collect appropriate objects: squeezy bottles and pebbles or dried peas (maracas); pieces of wood (wood blocks); large cardboard boxes and string (one-string bass); tubes and rice (rainmakers).

Many publications offer ideas on making instruments and the children are likely to have suggestions of their own. Encourage them to make instruments that will create interesting and unusual sounds.

##  Ideas bank

Clap a simple repeating rhythm. The children copy you. Change to a new, simple rhythm but the children may not copy your new rhythm until you say 'Fudge'. Once you are all clapping the same pattern again, change the rhythm once more. Any children who have a particularly good sense of rhythm could lead.

On any occasion, and for no particular reason, invite the children to sing a spontaneous song about what they have been doing. It might just be a song called 'A sunny day'. At this stage it may not sound too much like a song as we would know it, but it will bring together musical ideas.

Let the children use their voices to try to re-create sounds they have heard such as birdsong, a coffee percolator, a train arriving, an ambulance siren and so on. You could also use untuned percussion instruments to create sounds such as raindrops falling or footsteps, and tuned percussion instruments for the sound of a cuckoo, a donkey or clock chimes. Use these sounds in class music-making.

Invite any willing teachers, peripatetic instrumental teachers, helpers, parents or friends who play an instrument to come into school and give a very short demonstration. Ask them to join in by accompanying the children's singing.

Make sound charts with cut-out pictures stuck into columns which have the headings *High/ Low/Soft/Loud/Long/Short*. Some will fit into more than one column. Make this a point for discussion.

The children may well sing some of the old playground songs for skipping, ball games or circle games. 'Ring a roses' is a good example of the sound these songs all have. It is based on two notes which, in the tonic solfa, would be soh and me. On a piano, or another tuned instrument like chime bars, it could be G and E. Play these two notes over and over to the children and see if they can make up a simple song about a game they enjoy playing.

Sometimes use of a toy microphone will give confidence to a diffident singer or to someone with a speech difficulty.

# Assessment

The most important outcome of music making with young children is that they should have enjoyed it. This will be obvious at the end of any music session since children will want to sing, dance, clap or move on the way to their next activity. To help you evaluate whether or not you have achieved what you set out to do, the most important things in making music are to:

- get the children involved and encourage them to listen;
- let them perform;
- ask them what they think;
- give them lots of opportunities to create musical sounds and to put them together.

## What can they do?

- Listen attentively to sounds.
- Collect sounds.
- Recognise some differences in sounds.
- Recreate sounds.
- Use sounds.
- Respond to sounds.
- Discuss sounds.
- Sing a variety of songs.
- Play simple pieces of music on untuned instruments.
- Play simple accompaniments.
- Listen to short pieces of music.

## What have they experienced?

- Explored sounds, both vocal and instrumental.
- Used their bodies as instruments to make sounds.
- Handled and used untuned percussion instruments.
- Responded to music through dance, art and movement.
- Worked in small groups and as a whole class.
- Used the musical elements in their work.
- Gained some musical confidence.

## Can they perform?

Music making should be shared as much as possible with other people. Invite parents, carers, friends and peripatetic instrumental teachers to join in a music session and to make music together.

Whenever possible, the children should be encouraged to perform. A class assembly, presented to other children, is a particularly good way of sharing music making.

# Art

In Year 1 you need to build on the things which the children have explored and experienced in reception. Offer opportunities which will help to develop the children's visual perception and the skills that are needed for investigation and making. Your class should record responses to both the natural and made environment; gather and use resources and materials, use a range of materials and techniques, review and modify their work.

Introduce children to a range of work by artists, designers and craftspeople. The children should develop knowledge and understanding of the work of artists, craftspeople and designers and respond to, and comment on, art, craft and design.

## What should they be able to do?

By Year 1, children's fine motor ability will have developed through their experiences in the reception class and they should have increasing control of tools and materials for exploratory work as well as the ability to control shapes and pigments.

Most children will have passed through the stage where they produce random scribbled marks and will have developed their own collection of personal shapes and symbols. They will naturally repeat experiences, going over the same thing again and again until the idea is mastered. (These repeated shapes are known as the child's 'schema'.)

Some children will begin to show evidence of an analytical approach, matching shapes, lines, colours and so on to describe what they actually see, as well as continuing to use their spontaneous symbolic imagery. They are not necessarily confused by the use of the two approaches together in one picture.

But not all children of this age will be ready to respond in an analytical way so it is important to recognise this and appreciate each child's response. Personal imagery should, therefore, be respected, and continued opportunities should be given for symbolism, exploration and analysis.

Children in Year 1 can begin to work from observation as well as memory. Their developing awareness is best enhanced by offering rich opportunities for first-hand experience. Bring interesting things into the classroom and take the children out into the environment. Encourage lively discussion and use appropriate descriptive and challenging language.

Most children should have:

- had experience of a range of graphic materials;
- worked with thick paint;
- made simple prints;
- been introduced to tearing, cutting and sticking;
- modelled with materials in three dimensions.

If they have already done all these things, you should give them opportunities to consolidate and extend their experience. If not, you will have to begin with the most basic explorations.

Experiences in Year 1 should include:

- the use of tools and materials;
- work in the visual elements of art - pattern, texture, colour, line, tone, shape, form and space;
- visual communication and expression;
- a range of skills relating to the techniques of: drawing, painting, printing, collage, fabric work and work in 3D;
- introduction to pattern and colour in the work of other artists, craftspeople and designers, including at least one example from a non-western culture.

# Practical ideas

Starting points should be of genuine interest to the children, and should sometimes come spontaneously from them, perhaps when a member of the class has been involved in an important family event or brings in something interesting to show. In Year 1 items which relate to themselves (figures, houses, animals, flowers, vehicles and machines) are all of particular appeal.

Provide opportunities for looking at art and artefacts of all types, from detailed hard-edged work to the most extreme expressionist painting, from the figurative to abstract forms. This can widen children's horizons as well as informing you about their own expectations and interests.

They should be given the opportunity to work from their own ideas and imaginations. As well as working as a whole class, they should also sometimes work individually, and together in pairs or small groups.

## Making a start

### A well-organised environment

The whole classroom environment, from the pictures on the walls to the way in which the tools and materials are arranged and cared for, is part of the display and a statement about the way in which children's work is viewed and valued. This is a significant part of the teaching.

A lively and rich learning environment, with collections of visually exciting and tactile objects brought in by you and the children, will stimulate curiosity and encourage an interest in, and response to, the world at large.

### Tools and materials

Select a range of appropriate tools and materials of as good a quality as possible. They should suit the task but allow for an element of choice. Not all young children enjoy using thick paint and large brushes so, when working with paint, you could also offer finer brushes, water-colour paints or water-soluble crayons.

The proper way to care for tools and materials should be explained to the children from the beginning. Brushes should be washed and stored with the bristles pointing up. Spreaders for adhesive should be stored in plastic containers away from the brushes. It is best to supply water in a large ice-cream tub or a similar shallow container which is not easily knocked over. Paint, especially in ready-mix pots, can make quite an attractive feature if kept clean and stored tidily.

Plastic sweet jars provide good storage for coloured threads and small collage materials. The children might sort them into colour families. They can also sort fabrics into small open plastic storage trays for use in collage work or stitching activities. Flat trays also make good storage for water-colour boxes or packets of crayons. Plastic cutlery trays are useful for separating drawing materials of various kinds so that children can choose the one they want quickly.

## Images and artefacts

Encourage the children to bring interesting objects and artefacts into the classroom as this gives them a feeling of ownership. Collections of interesting items and artefacts can often be borrowed from museums too. These could be linked to a specific topic or theme and can be useful for extending children's experience.

Through discussion, using open ended questions, you can begin to help the children discover the potential of images, artefacts and collections as a source of ideas for their own work. If it is a picture, discuss the colours and the mood (happy, sad and so on). *What do you think is happening?* If it is an artefact, ask them to look at the shape and describe what it is. Talk about the colour. If it is not valuable, pass the object round and encourage the children to feel it carefully and describe the texture. They could draw or paint the object or use clay or junk materials to make something similar.

## Sources for images

Collect reproductions on postcards (and Christmas and birthday cards) from every possible source (some parents may be able to help) and put them in a photograph album in the book corner. You should be able to borrow art books with larger reproductions from the local library or the schools' library collection.(Give the library notice if you want a particular artist.) Sometimes art books and books with posters of artists' work can be found remaindered in bookshops. Out-of-date calendars of artists' work are also a good source.

# Introducing new key areas

## Investigating and making

For young children the materials themselves, if arranged in an enticing way, can provide a starting point. Lay out a range of colours, possibly grouping the reds and yellows together and the cooler colours of green and blue in another group.

Always encourage experimentation so that children have the opportunity to find out, within the bounds of reason and safety, what the tools and materials will do. However you will also need to teach specific techniques as well as ways of caring for tools and materials:

## Techniques
### Drawing

Provide well-sharpened drawing pencils 2B or 3B ('infant' pencils are also suitable). Give the children a small piece of paper and challenge them to see how many greys and blacks and how many patterns they can make. Straight afterwards they can do a drawing which offers possibilities for using greys, blacks and pattern. You could ask them to imagine a magic bird sitting on a nest. Describe the bird's feather patterns and the twigs in the nest.

## Painting

Provide ready-mix paint in plastic bun tins. Show the children how to lift small quantities of paint either directly on to the paper or on to a mixing palette if they want to make a different colour. Show them how to rinse their brushes and get rid of any excess water by wiping them. (Provide a few sheets of newspaper cut small for this and hang a dustbin bag over the back of a chair for the used newspaper.)

Introduce observational work from both the natural and made world. You could bring in a bunch of flowers and put it in a pot against a contrasting background. Discuss colours and shapes, perhaps looking at paintings of flowers in vases by Odilon Redon or Henri Matisse. Then ask the children to do a painting of the flowers.

Put a number of soft toys into a group. Talk together about the shapes and the characters of the toys. Emphasise the need to look at their expressions.( It could be useful to show and read one of the 'Old Bear' stories by Jane Hissey as the illustrations of the characters are particularly good.) Ask the children to paint or draw the group.

## Printing

Provide paper, a box of small objects (cotton reels, cogs, wooden blocks and so on) and plastic trays with a small amount of paint in the middle. Then place a piece of flat cleaning sponge (about 1cm

thick) over the paint. When the children press the objects on to the sponge they will be coated with the right amount of paint.

Encourage them to see how many prints they can make without re-loading the object and to experiment with colour, finding out what happens if they print one colour over another. Discuss and display the results.

## Collage

Provide adhesive, scissors and a selection of small pieces of paper of varying colours, pattern and texture and a range of small pieces of interesting fabric. (Plastic cutlery trays will encourage children to keep the materials organised as they work.) This is a good opportunity to talk about colour and texture.

As a starting point, you could read one of the 'Elmer' stories by David McKee. Elmer is an elephant who is made of patchwork. The children could then make Elmer or just work directly with the materials, using colours and textures that they like. They could add paint to some areas of the collage.

## Modelling

Provide opportunities for working with malleable materials like clay and Plasticine and with 'junk' materials. Use PVA glue for junk modelling and show children how to use small amounts on their spreaders. (Adhesive can be stored and used in the small, lidded pots which hold photographic film.)

You do not need to have a working kiln to experiment with clay. The experience of making does not depend on the models becoming a permanent item, the value lies in the practical making task.

However, if you want to keep the results, you can use fibre-reinforced clay which does not need a kiln. It dries in the air and can then be painted with thick paint and varnished.

## Vocabulary

It is important to introduce appropriate language to the children. They should be motivated and encouraged through open-ended questions and discussion to communicate their opinions and observations about their own, and other artists', work. Use words such as explore, record, imagine and describe, in appropriate contexts when you are talking to the children.

## Explore

Exploration may sometimes be by trial and error, and sometimes through guided discovery. Children could, for example, make a painting and, when it is dry, draw into it with pastels. Or they could paint a picture and add collage (bits of material and paper) then paint on top again.

Give each child a pencil, a crayon, chalk and a piece of paper divided up into sections. (A sketchbook is an ideal place for this activity.) *Explore the different kinds of mark, lights and darknesses which you can make with one tool. Then see what happens when you use chalk and crayon in the same drawing.*

Offer two primary colours (red and yellow, blue and yellow, blue and red) plus white. Also hog hair brushes, mixing palettes and small square pieces of white cartridge paper. *How many different-coloured stripes can you make on this piece of paper?* Display the results edge to edge like a patchwork as part of a general display on the topic of colour.

Give each child a ball of clay or soft Plasticine about the size of a tennis ball. *What happens when you squeeze, roll, pull...?* (If they work on a small board or piece of sugar paper, the clay won't stick to the table.)

## Sketchbooks

The National Curriculum requires children to work with sketchbooks at KS2 but it is valuable for children to become familiar with this way of working from the beginning. (Any plain paper stitched or stapled makes a sketchbook.) One of

the advantages is that you have a record of the way in which the children are exploring techniques. Experiments on small loose pieces of paper tend to get lost.

If the children are already using newsbooks these make an ideal place in which to experiment with different tools and materials. They are also useful for recording things outside, such as simple drawings on a visit to a nature centre, or in the school grounds. You can also prompt children by asking them to think of things they have done, getting them to close their eyes and picture the scene as if they were standing in front of it.

## The elements of art

Provide opportunities for experimentation with the elements of art: line, colour, shape, pattern, texture, form. It is rare for a work of art to have only one element in its make up and children will usually be working with several of the elements in one piece of work. You could read the story of 'The Quangle Wangle's Hat' by Edward Lear and ask the children to imagine someone in a magic hat which is full of birds, flowers and insects. A painting of this hat could involve line, pattern, tone, colour, shape and texture. This particular story could also lend itself to a large class picture with each of the children painting one thing to put on the hat.

# Themes

There are many projects (see suggestions below) which can be interpreted purely for art, or in a cross-curricular manner, where factual and creative writing, prose and poetry, drama, movement and, sometimes, other subject areas such as history or mathematics can play a role.

## Portraits

One good theme is portraits. Organise a class portrait gallery. Ask the children to bring in family photos/portraits. (Try to obtain some formal photographs taken at the end of the last century.) Discuss how portraits can be full length, half length, or head and shoulders and find examples among the photographs. *What differences do you notice between the old photographs and the modern ones?*

Explain how portraits can be a record of how people looked long ago before photography was invented. Look at reproductions of portraits by

Gainsborough, Rembrandt, Velasquez and so on. (Use paintings which show children as well as adults.) Link this with work in history as they discuss the clothes the people are wearing and the different ways in which children were dressed long ago. *How are painted portraits different from photographs?* Then ask them to draw or paint a portrait, from memory, of a friend or a member of their family, wearing their favourite clothes. Hang these in the portrait gallery.

Show the class a reproduction of a self-portrait by an artist. Van Gogh would be suitable but there are many to choose from. Ask: *Can you describe the person in the picture? Is he/she sad/happy old/young?*. Ask them to imagine that they are famous artists. *Can you paint a self portrait so that people will know what you look like?* You could ask them what they would like to have with them in their portrait to show their interests or what sort of person they are, perhaps a pet, a special possession or something to indicate a favourite hobby. It may be useful to look at portraits by Hockney and Freud.

Look at the way in which various artists have used colour to portray character, Van Gogh, Picasso, Derain and Matisse would be suitable. This is a good opportunity for some children to dress up, alternatively you could invite an adult to come in, dressed in some special colourful clothes, to model for the children.

## Weather

For a non-figurative theme, you could look at the weather.(Perhaps in conjunction with work in geography.) Look at artists' depictions of the weather and ways of using materials, techniques and the elements of art to create different moods. Constable and Turner are useful examples. You could also look at Van Gogh and the German Expressionist artist, Nolde, before allowing the children to try out their own ways of depicting the weather.

## Reviewing

Spend time sitting alongside children so that they can talk with you about what they are doing. By discussing their work, they will learn to reflect on it, to modify it and suggest new ideas. Ask them to choose their best piece of work and to tell you why they like it or perhaps how they could change it.

This is also an opportunity to reinforce vocabulary related to new experiences, elements, tools or techniques. For example, ask them to point out where they have mixed colours in their work and ask what they used.

## Display

Display is one of the ways in which we evaluate children's work. Involve the children as much as possible in making decisions about the way in which their work is displayed and try to include everybody's work in the display. Sometimes a 'pavement show', laying out the work on the hall floor, or pinning it up quickly so that it can be celebrated and talked about immediately is a valuable exercise. It is a way of building on the children's experiences and making teaching points while the experience is still fresh in their minds.

## Knowledge and understanding

Use your collection of reproductions to introduce children to colourful abstract images, pictures with story content and to three dimensional-forms.

Children can be encouraged to describe a variety of images and artefacts, to voice likes and dislikes and make choices about which they like best. This can take place through whole-class discussions, group work or spontaneously on an individual basis.

They can begin to recognise the elements of art in the work of other artists, craftspeople and designers and apply this knowledge to their own work, perhaps by looking at other artists' use of colour and responding by using colour vigorously in their own work.

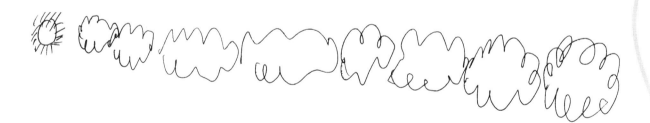

# Developing key areas

## Recording what has been observed and imagined

### Approaches

▶ **My family** – *who are they, what do they wear, what do they look like, how do they behave, what colours can you use?*

▶ **Where I live** – *what is it made of, what shapes are in it: windows, doors, chimneys, colours, patterns of bricks, tiles and so on?*

▶ A **baby** – from their own family or a friend's, from imagination.

▶ A **pet** or an animal they own or know well – *think of the way it looks, feels, moves and its character.*

▶ A **favourite moment** or event – during a visit to the beach/park/shops.

▶ A **favourite toy** – *think of feeling it, looking at it, playing with it, what it is made of, shapes.*

## Images and artefacts as sources of ideas

▶ A collection, for example, each child brings in a favourite toy.

▶ Showing them something unusual, exciting or surprising, such as an artefact from another country, an unusual fruit or an exotic flower.

▶ Taking them out, to a farm park, the beach or a small local museum.

▶ Finding a story related to your chosen focus.

▶ Using music/songs as extra stimulus.

### Observations and comments

▶ *Who can tell me what this is?*

▶ *Who can see a ... ?*

▶ *Is it large or small?*

▶ *What shape is it?*

▶ *What colour is it?*

▶ *Do you think it feels rough or smooth? How can you tell?*

▶ *Can you draw it in the air with your finger?*

### Evidence of success

▶ Interest and motivation.

▶ Ability to observe form, texture, colour shape and so on.

▶ Vocabulary - smooth, soft, hairy, shiny, rough, bright and so on.

▶ Personal response – likes, dislikes and so on.

▶ Searching for, and selecting from, resources and ideas.

## Tools, materials, techniques and the visual elements

### Approaches

▶ Placing the object against a background.

▶ Experimenting – making a range of different marks with paint, mixing different colours.

▶ Using different kinds of paint, such as paint with PVA glue added.

▶ Offering a range of tools, for example cotton buds, sticks, big and small brushes.

### Observations and comments

▶ *What marks can you make with crayon/paint which will look like...?*

▶ *Which tool did you use to make this mark?*

▶ *Which brush can you use to make a tiny/big mark?*

▶ *Which tool/paint are you going to choose to make the ....?*

▶ *Which mark do you like best?*

▶ *Why do you like it?*

▶ *Which mark looks like...?*

▶ *Can you mix a different colour?*

▶ *What colours did you use to make your new colour? Can you do it again?*

### Evidence of success

▶ A willingness to try new things.

▶ Personal response and choice.

▶ Visual and tactile awareness.

▶ Markmaking of all kinds.

▶ Beginnings of colour mixing.

▶ Awareness of texture.

▶ Involvement and concentration.

▶ Use of appropriate descriptive vocabulary.

## Artists, craftsmen and designers

### Approaches

▶ Bringing in examples or reproductions of a range of art.

▶ Selecting reproductions of abstract art with bright colours.

▶ Selecting art with objects beginning with particular letters of the alphabet.

▶ Selecting pictures with several images of the same object for the children to identify and count.

(Postcards or calendars are a useful resource.)

## Observations and comments
◗ *Which picture do you like best?*
◗ *What colours can you see?*
◗ *Can you see something in the picture beginning with ...?*
◗ *How many ... can you see in the picture?*

## Evidence to look for
◗ Personal likes and dislikes.
◗ Awareness of detail, such as colour, shape, texture and so on.

## Artists, craftsmen and designers from other cultures, individual artists

### Approaches
◗ Introducing a famous artist, for example, the colourful work of Van Gogh, Matisse or Howard Hodgkin.
◗ Introducing patterns from other cultures, for example, aboriginal pattern.

### Observations and comments
◗ *Can anybody tell me the name of a famous artist ?*

◗ *The name of the artist who painted this picture is ...*
◗ *What do you think the artist used to make this picture?*
◗ *Can anybody tell me the name of a place where you can see lots of paintings?*
◗ *Can anybody tell me what sort of patterns these are? Which country do you think these patterns come from?*

### Evidence of success
◗ The beginning of an awareness that there are different ways of making art in two and three dimensions.
◗ Awareness that there are lots of different kinds of pictures, that galleries are places where artists' work can be seen and that people all over the world make art, craft and design.

## Responding and describing

### Approaches
◗ Making printed patterns using small found objects (for example cotton reels, small cogs and other mechanical parts, blocks of wood) dipped in paint as printing tools.
◗ Looking at colour in artists' work and responding by using it vigorously in their own work.
◗ Creating a class gallery.

### Observations and comments
◗ *What colours can you see?*
◗ *Which colour do you like best?*
◗ *How many different colours can you find?*
◗ *Can you make some of those colours?*
◗ *What colours would you use?*

### Evidence of success
◗ Likes and dislikes.
◗ Colour recognition.
◗ The beginning of colour mixing.
◗ Personal motivation and response.
◗ Independent thinking.

## ✤Ideas bank
### Wall display
The 'unit' approach makes a striking display but allows each child to retain part of it afterwards. Each child makes or paints an object or image which is a unit for a large wall or table display,

perhaps figures for a tableau or family group. Each child's unit should be of his or her own devising and should be based on observation, rather than a template, which is a poor substitute for lively originality and gives a very flat result.

## Greetings cards

▶ Fold a piece of card carefully;

▶ choose a size for children's work;

▶ guide the childrens' choice of image, but allow them to make a personal statement – perhaps a pattern based on pattern from another culture, a small piece of paper weaving or rubbings;

▶ select appropriate tools and materials;

▶ sometimes choose to restrict colour;

▶ use collage, painting, drawing, print;

▶ encourage children to write their own messages in the cards, perhaps in coloured pen or crayon;

▶ try something 3D, such as a self portrait drawn into a rolled out rectangle of clay, cut out, fired in the kiln and stuck on to a thick piece of card, with a message written underneath by the child.

## ❋ Assessment

In Year 1, children's interpretations of what they see may be symbolic, moving towards the visually real, and in many cases the imagery is still more to do with what they know than what they see.

It is important to respond sensitively to the questions they ask, the things they say, what they do and what they give us.

A vital consideration in any evaluation of outcomes in art is respect for personal and cultural identity, particularly as art should be instrumental in developing self-confidence. It is also important to develop positive attitudes to art through praise, help and encouragement.

It is, however, possible to evaluate some of the following aspects of the children's endeavours in art at this stage:

● *How have they used what they have been given?*

● *What have they done and what are they trying to do?*

● *What evidence do we see of independent thinking and personal ideas?*

● *Have they been willing to experiment?*

● *Are they developing a knowledge of how tools and materials behave?*

● *Have the materials been used in an imaginative way?*

● *Have they begun to mix colours?*

● *Have they learned a new skill/technique?*

● *Are they beginning to understand the context of art, artists, galleries?*

● *Have they learned about art from another country/culture/period?*

● *Are they growing more confident?*

● *Are they motivated and involved?*

● *Can they work co-operatively?*

# Physical Education

Your Year 1 class may be familiar with the routine for PE, (changing, where to put clothes and going to the hall or playground) but you will need to explain and establish your own special requirements (what to do when they are ready, how to line up, and so on). They should be becoming more independent and more used to responding as a class, but it is still helpful to provide a consistent and regular routine.

In many schools, PE is timetabled three times a week. For your class this will usually mean one session for gymnastic-type activities with large apparatus, one session for dance and one for games activities.

Sometimes you could use these time-tabled periods more flexibly, but make sure you maintain the balance of the three activities throughout the term/year. If you only have two timetabled sessions in the hall you must choose when in the year you will teach each of the activities, although in addition to hall times you will often be able to take the children outside for games when the weather permits. Try also to use spontaneous opportunities for movement (such as action rhymes and games) in addition to the regular PE times.

Short, purposeful sessions are most beneficial. Use opportunities to develop other aspects of children's learning (perhaps language or mathematics ) through their physical activities.

## What should they be able to do?

When the children come into your class you will be aware of vast differences in their experience, interest, physique, temperament, attitude and effort. Whatever experiences they have had outside school or in the reception class, they will need help and encouragement to move safely with others, on apparatus or with equipment, using all the available space.

Many children will still need practice in managing their bodies to stop and start their actions. They will all enjoy playing 'statue' type games which will sharpen their listening and response and, by the end of the year, they should all be more successful in controlling their bodies to come to a halt when asked to do so.

All children will be able to walk, run, gallop, hop and jump (apart from those with specific physical impairments) with increasing control and awareness and many will have a wider range of actions which they can perform successfully. By the end of the year they should be beginning to clarify or refine their own actions, (bending their knees on landing, stretching their ankles more) when asked to do so, and some will do so without prompting. Encourage the children to walk tall, run on their toes and use their arms in opposition as they walk.

As they practise these actions in different ways (slowly and carefully, energetically) in Dance, Gymnastics or Games they will begin to recognise and understand the effect of exercise on their bodies, (feeling hotter, breathing faster and getting tired quickly). Although the sequence of progression through the stages of motor development is the same for most children, they do not progress at the same rate, or at an even rate, so there will be a wide range of differences in the ways children in your class achieve various actions or movements.

## Key area: Dance

Your class will show awareness of some body parts and will be increasingly able to isolate different parts and move them in time with the music or sounds. Some children will be able to do this confidently and quickly with increasing control and co-ordination, while others will need lots of encouragement to join in and try the movements fully.

They will show a growing ability to use their imagination, to listen and respond to the music or rhythm, to observe and copy the actions of others or to contribute ideas of their own. They will be developing control and fluency when performing basic actions like stepping, creeping, hopping and jumping and should be able to respond to variations in speed (slowly/quickly), strength (lightly/strongly) and fluency (smoothly/jerkily) as indicated by clear, simple accompaniment. They should be encouraged to side-step and skip, and will be developing their ability to do this rhythmically and continuously in time to music. They should be getting better at making full use of the space and using different pathways (curving, straight), but will still need help to do so.

They will have some understanding of direction, size and level and be able to choose a different direction in which to move or a different level to start when asked to do so, but this will need to be developed. Using contrasting actions is an excellent way to heighten the experiences for them (high/low, near/far, shrinking/stretching).

## Key area: Gymnastics

Most children will be agile and adventurous, but while some may need lots of encouragement, others may need help in becoming more cautious and aware of others. All of the children will need plenty of time to try out and practise their walking, running, jumping, sliding, rolling, crawling and climbing actions and to try them in different situations, some on parts of the apparatus.

They will probably be able to jump from one foot to two feet, two feet to two feet and one foot to the other foot. They will be coming more proficient at moving from one foot to

the same foot (hop). Encourage them to use the non-dominant foot as often as possible or suggest times to change over. With regular practice, in non-threatening situations, you will notice an improvement in skill and confidence with their developing strength and balance.

Most of them should be able to sustain still, clear shapes on large parts of their bodies (back, sides, tummy, and on two feet and all fours). Gradually, they should be able to show you that they can do this on smaller parts of their bodies (seat, one foot, shoulders, two hands and one foot). With hands flat on the floor and arms straight (as they hold still shapes or move on their hands and feet) and by holding or hanging on apparatus they will begin to develop confidence and strength in their upper bodies.

## Key area: Games

At the start of the year most children will need to be encouraged to find spaces and to use the available space to develop their awareness of others. They will continue to need reminders, particularly when using equipment. They will be able to play alongside each other but will need your encouragement and help to share and take turns.

With regular practice, by the end of the year most children should be able to:

- take responsibility for looking after the equipment efficiently;
- select from a limited range of equipment and follow instructions;
- release and guide (roll, tap, throw, kick) a ball, sending it with increasing accuracy towards a still target (between skittles, into a hoop, to a partner, or between markings on the floor or wall). They should be encouraged to take time to aim and should know that they need to keep their eyes on the target and follow through in the direction they want the ball to go;
- stop a ball when it is rolled to them (slowly and often quickly);
- catch a large ball or beanbag by bringing it into their chests, relying less and less on the body and more on just their hands (with varying degrees of success);
- bounce and catch a ball with two hands in several positions (sitting, kneeling, standing, moving slowly) and count the number of times they can do so. Many will enjoy tap-bouncing a large or medium ball, using the hand as a bat, and will be working towards doing this consistently. They should be given opportunities to co-operate and work together, to share equipment and take turns. Most will do this fairly when encouraged and helped to do so.

# Practical ideas

## 🌸 Making a start

### Dance

#### Different ways to start
● Clapping, stamping, tapping and counting to a simple rhythm (perhaps in time to the beat of a tambourine).

● Moving, shaking, touching, and identifying different part of their bodies (wiggling fingers, shrugging shoulders, circling ankles).

● Develop and practise travelling actions in short phrases (walking, slow stepping, marching, creeping, stamping, skipping, tip-toeing, striding) with various forms of accompaniment, (percussion, music or voice). Encourage variations (perhaps one phrase in one direction, one in another; one moving near the ground, one up high).

● Use phrases of 16 or 8 beats on the spot and/or moving.
This will help your class use the space, try different actions, respond to the rhythm and gradually raise the heart beat.

#### Topic
Use characters or ideas from your topic (for example crooked man, space walk, monster stomp), and emphasise the important qualities (such as shape, weightlessness, strength). You could, for example, try out crooked shapes with different parts of the body (arms or legs), with the whole body, with crooked pathways, contrasting these with very direct pathways and shapes to emphasise and highlight the differences. Build phrases into a sequence to create a short dance.

#### Body parts dance
Focus on selected body parts for a dance: hands and knees, hips and hands, elbows and feet, fingers and toes. Explore the different ways each part can be moved (shaken, stretched, tapped) and then put together in a phrase of actions (such as shake, shake, shake, tap, tap, tap, tap, s t r e t

c h...apart slowly.. back together suddenly) using percussion as accompaniment.
Encourage relaxation and cooling down by using slow swaying music, music for slow walking, or simply calm music to sit/lie and listen to.

### Gymnastics

Help children to think about their actions by selecting a focus or theme, such as travelling or balancing. Try out ideas in the floorwork part of the lesson and then on the apparatus. Whatever the theme, children will need to be taught to handle and use the apparatus carefully, so emphasise the safety factors.

#### Organisation of apparatus
● Divide the class into five or six groups.

● Check all apparatus fixings and placement before the children use it.

● Establish 'ground rules' (looking where you are going, keep in a space, do not get too close to others).

● Insist on a quiet working atmosphere, but discuss with the children why this is important.

● Encourage and help the children to share space and equipment (using the floor space around the apparatus), particularly when the amount of apparatus is limited.

● Establish a consistent routine for stopping, coming down and sitting away from the apparatus.

## Travelling

● Encourage children to try different ways of moving on their feet (hopping, jogging, walking, jumping), hands and feet (crawling, bunny jumping) and body parts (sliding, rolling sideways) to travel around the floor. Help them become more aware of the ways they can clarify and refine their body actions. *I liked the way you used your arms to help you jump/stretched on your tummy/ went backwards under the plank on your back*), and give them opportunities to choose and select appropriate movements.

● Reinforce teaching of jumping and landing (softly and safely, bending at the knees, hips and ankles), and check that hands are flat on the floor when moving on hands and feet.

● Encourage children to focus on travelling actions as they move around the apparatus. Stress moving into spaces and suggest that they try different ways of travelling around, on and off, over and under the apparatus.

## Balancing

To develop balancing, help children to clarify still shapes on large parts (backs, sides, tummies) and smaller parts of the body (two feet, one foot, hands and feet, seats, shoulders). Encourage them to hold the shape for the count of three before moving to a new space and trying another still shape. In this way they will be moving in their own time and in control of their actions.

● Each group should be responsible for handling the same apparatus each lesson. (Change over each term.)

● Make a plan of the apparatus to be used, which will support the theme (for example more flat and separate surfaces for balancing).

● Establish a fair and logical pattern of rotation of groups (perhaps zigzag, clockwise, or a straight swap if there are groups with similar apparatus) so that, over a period of several lessons, the children can explore fully each group of apparatus in turn. (There should only be a maximum of two apparatus changes in one lesson.)

● Teach each group how to get out their piece of apparatus (spaced out around the apparatus, bending their knees rather than their backs, holding on, all looking in the direction in which they are carrying the apparatus) and where to put it. (Use chalk marks initially to help indicate the positioning of the apparatus.)

# Games

## Class games

Introduce and use a variety of class games to start and/or finish the lesson. Start with familiar games like 'Statues' or 'Traffic Lights' and gradually introduce new ones like the 'Bean Game' (Children perform the action indicated by the type of bean called out: runner bean (run), broad bean (wide shape), jelly bean (shake), baked bean (lie on back with legs in the air), dwarf bean (walk in crouched position )or 'This Way and That' (They stand in a long line facing you. Indicate *That Way* (to the right) or *This Way* (to the left). Change the command frequently so they have to change direction quickly.) This will encourage listening, quick responses to your stop and start commands and will give them the opportunity to become more aware of the space and others as they move.

Use a variety of actions in fun situations where they have no fear of being 'out' and they will gradually become more competent in their actions.

Begin to focus on specific actions for part of the lesson to help children develop new skills.

## Equipment

The children will have been introduced to a variety of equipment in the reception class, but they will still need your guidance in exploring and practising different ways of manipulating and using it.

Allow time for lots of individual practice and include some challenges and some suggestions.

### Beanbags

- Carry and pass the beanbag on the move.

- Try to catch and throw the beanbag in pairs, starting very close together, (catcher has cupped hands ready and, with gentle throws, the thrower tries to place the beanbag in the catcher's hands).

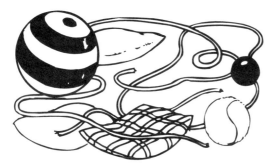

### Jumping with ropes

- Jump over and in and out of their rope shapes on the floor - this will develop the stamina and rhythm needed to skip with a rope.

- Run in and out of the shapes on the floor without touching them, jump over them and return to their starting shape on the stop signal.

- Work in threes, two children sway the rope gently and one jumps over it (side to side or forwards and backwards).Remind them to take turns fairly.

- Walk, turn and step over a rope individually. Some children may be able to skip so introduce challenges (*how many? a little faster, backwards*).

- Choice of jumping with rope (perhaps a pattern on the floor, a swaying rope or skipping).

### Large and small balls

- Make a game of passing a small ball around the body, in different directions.

- Roll and stop a ball in different ways (with two hands, one hand, two feet, one foot ...).

- In larger spaces, chase and collect, and chase and stop the ball.

- Drop/bounce the ball and catch it with two hands (high, low).

- Throw it up, let it bounce and catch it.

**Dribbling** – use little taps with hand or foot (or maybe other parts of the body), along the ground. Use changes of direction (*and change!... and change!*) to encourage listening, responding and controlling. Follow pathways (zigzag, curving), or make patterns on the floor.

**Safety** – Remind children that if they are moving backwards they must look where they are going.

Establish safe and responsible use of equipment by training the children to take care of it (putting it out, putting it away and checking that all apparatus has been neatly returned to the baskets). Colour coding of equipment and counting will help to ensure that apparatus is not left lying about and lost.

# ❀ Developing key areas

## Dance

### Rhythm, body awareness and travelling actions

● Make travelling actions fun, with changes in tempo (getting slightly faster or slower) or changes in strength (lightly, quietly, or strongly).

● Use a variety of music to develop children's dancing and listening skills (for example 'The Grand Old Duke of York' (marching); the Peter theme, from *Peter and the Wolf* (skipping) and 'Floating in the Air' from *The Snowman* for floating movements.

● Focus on the essential qualities of how each of the actions is performed - strongly, quickly, smoothly.

● Percussion can provide a clear stimulus for actions and each instrument can suggest several qualities (a strong drum beat for marching or stamping, a light tap for tiptoeing; shaking a tambourine for wriggling, scraping for twisting, tapping for light running). Build phrases of actions with contrasting strength, speed or level.

### Action words

● Use words which enhance both the children's language and dance experiences (wriggle, stamp, bounce, float, collapse).

● Help them refine their actions through the use of words, and the way they are said (*s - l - o - w - l- y, st - r - e - t - ch* or *halt!*).

● Develop the actions into phrases for the climax of the lesson so children can begin to feel the idea of a beginning, middle and end to a dance (for example *cre - e - e - ep... explode!* and *melt*).

● Develop both word and action vocabulary by exploring action words and the different qualities they suggest (travelling - *drift, rush, stride; wriggle, slide;* jumping - *leap, toss;* gesturing - *shiver, shake, shrink;* stopping - *flop, halt, pause;* turning - *whirl, spin.*

● Specifically encourage moving at different levels (high, medium, low), in different directions (forwards, sideways, backwards, up and down) and using different pathways (straight, curving, zigzag), as children move around the hall.

### Stories

Often, in a story, reference is made to an action such as walking on the moon, crawling through the jungle, casting spells and so on, and these can be explored in dance. Develop them into phrases of action (*step and step and step and stop, turn and look at the moon surface, try jumping as if you are weightless and step, step and step back to the rocket*).

● Tell stories through movement (squeeze through a narrow then low tunnel, wade through a swamp, balance on a tightrope).

### Objects

● These provide a focus of attention and a rich source of language and stimulation for movement. *Imagine you are an elastic band – limp and crumpled; stretch in one direction slowly, stretch in another slowly, (up and down, in front, behind) stretch quickly and snap back to your crumpled shape. Try this continuously and jerkily.*

### Develop responses

The more you observe the children's responses, the more ways you will find to develop creative, expressive forms of dance.

● Introduce partner work by encouraging one child to move and another to watch (for short times) or follow-my-leader activities where one leads, while the other copies, and then the roles are reversed.

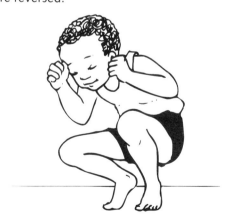

● Praise interesting ideas and ask the children to move again to make part of the action clearer. *I liked the way you used all parts of your body while you shivered.*

● Encourage them to exaggerate the actions and to use their whole body when appropriate.

● Provide lots of contrasting actions (leap and sprawl) and qualities (smoothly or jerkily) which will heighten the experiences for the children and help them recognise and really feel the differences.

● Provide a framework within which they can work by using phrases of accompaniment with voice or percussion, or short pieces of music to suit their concentration and to enable them to remember, repeat, refine and perform their dancing actions.

● Encourage appreciation of the work of others by watching a partner, then changing over, or asking half the class to watch the other half, then changing over.

# Gymnastics
## Themes

Use a focus or theme, rather than specific skills, to introduce a new aspect of movement to your class. This will encourage the children to think about their movements and try different actions.

Children will still need encouragement to use the space well, particularly on the apparatus. It is helpful if they start on apparatus on which they are confident, providing there is a space, and are then encouraged to try different pieces of apparatus.

### Directions

Children should experiment with travelling forwards, sideways and backwards showing awareness of others and the apparatus, using feet, hands and feet and body parts.

### Together and apart

Thinking about when their feet are together or apart will help children to consider different ways of balancing and travelling. At the end of a series of lessons they can be asked to choose their favourite ways of moving, with their feet apart and/or together.

### Prepositions

Encourage varied use of the apparatus by thinking of travelling *around, towards, away from, on and off, over and under* it, using feet, hands and feet, and body parts.

### Using hands

Help children to be more aware of their hands - to take their weight, help them balance and jump, to climb, to hang, to push along.

# Games
## Ball handling

● Develop bouncing and dribbling skills by suggesting variations to challenge individuals or groups (such as high, low; two hands, one hand; alternate hands or feet; using large, medium and small balls; making patterns; moving slowly).

● Try rolling, stopping and striking possibly using hand(s) as a bat or using a medium bat (such as a padder tennis bat).

● Inventing games (*Make up a game which includes bouncing a ball on your own/with your*

*partner*). Make sure of fair turns. Working with a partner to invent a game will give the children in your class the opportunity to observe others, plan and collaborate with each other and describe what they want to do.

## Challenges

● Introduce challenges within a chosen or specified activity. *How many? Can you beat your own record?*

● Challenge the children to combine actions, such as running and jumping: over lines, shapes, beanbags or ropes in the hall or playground, making hopscotch-type patterns, or playing 'widening river'. (Make a 'v' shape with a rope. Begin by jumping over the pointed end, then gradually jump towards the wider open end.)

● It is important to allow some opportunities for free play within each lesson as this will allow children to choose and practise with pieces of equipment and work at their own level. However, it is helpful if you also specifically challenge them to try a range of different actions to increase their movement vocabulary, or to make the actions in which they are confident more difficult. *Use the other hand/foot. Try to bounce the ball in a different position/as you are moving along/a bit further away/a bit higher.*)

● Develop shared, co-operative challenges. Provide opportunities for made-up games in pairs using a specified or chosen piece of equipment. *Make a pattern of bounces with your ball (two*

*hands, one hand, two hands/two bounces there, two bounces here/ beat your record).* Alternatively make up a game using a specified action, perhaps rolling, stopping or bouncing. This allows children to be inventive, use their initiative, share ideas and practise their skills. They begin to become aware of the fundamentals of games play in a situation where they are in control.

Challenges like these are an introduction to simple competitive games. Each child is encouraged to try harder and make the action more difficult without the disappointment of not being first, or not getting the highest number.

## Ideas bank

### Dance

● Use stories as a stimulus for movement, perhaps the story of a haunted house (ghosts, making frightening shapes, being frightened, hiding) or one of the *Funny Bones books* by Allan Ahlberg (skeletons walking, jumping, turning, running and hiding).

● Read the children poems which suggest movement. Ask them to express specific descriptive action words, encouraging their movements to become larger than life.

● Listen to the tapes of BBC dance programmes to select a movement or thematic focus. Then use the accompaniment and develop the ideas in your own way, with your own class, rather than using the voice on the tape.

### Gymnastics

Ask children to:

● Choose their favourite ways of moving (on all fours, on their sides, stretched shapes) and to repeat them, trying to find ways to make them better.

● Select specific types of movements (wide shapes on hands and feet, travelling on backs or tummies with feet together) to encourage them to think about which actions are appropriate.

● Link movements – link one way of travelling on hands and feet with one way of travelling on another part of the body, or choose a travelling action, a balance and a jump and practise them one after the other.

## Games

● Provide opportunities for made-up games in pairs using a specified or chosen piece of equipment (for example one hoop and one ball between two), or a specified action (for example dribbling, stopping or bouncing).

● As children become more adept at stopping, starting and changing direction, they can be encouraged to do this more quickly with variations in speed (getting faster, stopping suddenly).

● Use grids or playground markings to help with spacing.

● Use hoops or rope shapes on the floor. Children will then have their own space to return to, to stand or sit in, to bounce their ball or spin their ball or quoit in, and to provide a target or focus for their actions.

# Assessment

Because of the fleeting nature of physical actions, detailed observation of a class of children constantly on the move is difficult. However it is a good idea for you to get a general impression or overall feel for the class response before looking more specifically at the movement of individual children. Ask yourself questions such as:

- How do the children respond, listen to my instructions/suggestions?
- How well do they think for themselves/follow others/do a bit of both?
- How well do they use the space? How could they be encouraged to use it better?
- Are they able to use different directions? Are they aware of others when they do so? What could I say that might help them?
- How well do they sustain energetic activity? Can they talk about and describe some of their actions and experiences in PE?
- Are there other observations I need to make?

Then try to watch how individual children respond and move. Continual review of the class with a focus on a few children at a time is recommended. There will also be times when you note achievement which is particularly significant for one child, or the class, or look for specific actions or responses.

- Do they use the whole of the body when required?
- Which parts could they make more use of?
- How controlled are their movements?
- In which ways could they refine their movements - is the fluency of the action easy or awkward?

At this age children may still be inconsistent in their actions so watch for times when they may substitute one travelling action for another (perhaps a gallop instead of a skip), and praise their attempts to learn a new skill.

## Dance

- How well do they respond to my voice, the rhythm, sounds or music?
- How imaginative/creative are they?
- Are they achieving the qualities required? When? If not, why not? What might help?
- How well can they isolate and use individual body parts? Do they use some parts more fully than others?
- Do they use different levels of their own volition?
- How well do they remember a phrase or sequence of movements?
- Can they choose their own starting positions from options suggested?

## Gymnastics

- How well do they use the apparatus? Are there pieces of apparatus which I need to encourage them to use?

- How inventive are their actions?
- Can they hold still shapes on large and small parts of their bodies for the count of three?
- How confidently can they take their weight on their hands (on all fours, bunny jumps)?

● Can they choose, repeat and refine their favourite movements and select appropriate actions?

● Can they remember two (or three actions) and perform them one after the other?

## Games

● How well do they move about the space in different directions and in different ways?

● Can they stop, start and weave in and out of each other?

● Can they use the equipment imaginatively and confidently in a variety of ways?

● How accurately can they roll or throw towards a stationary target?

At all times stress the positive aspects of the children's movement and enjoy and encourage their attempts. There will be as many different responses as there are children. Remember that sometimes excitement, stress or the many demands of a situation, particularly in games, will cause some children to use less advanced movements.

# Information Technology

Much of the Information Technology work you do with Year 1 children will be getting them used to using the computer effectively. This involves introducing them to the three main input devices – the keyboard, overlay keyboard and mouse – in a carefully-structured way. You should, however, make sure you are aware of the experiences that the children have had, both in the reception class and at home, and give them opportunities to build upon their existing skills.

Although the keyboard is generally the most common way of putting information into a computer, some Year 1 children may have problems with pressing the keys effectively and with recognising upper-case letters. However, some suppliers (such as RM) now provide replacement keyboards with lower-case letters that may be more appropriate for some of your class. It is also possible to cover keys with stickers on which the lower-case letters have been written.

An overlay keyboard (such as the concept keyboard) allows you to customise the input device so that, instead of pressing individual letters, sections of the keyboard can be designated as whole words, or even as a drawing and, when they are pressed, the appropriate word will appear on the screen.

(Artwork and caption)

To use the mouse effectively requires considerable skill and practice. Children should be aware of the link between the movement of the mouse in their hand, and the movement of the pointer on the screen. They should also be taught how clicking the mouse button (usually the one on the left) is used to select something on the screen. In many programs it is possible to slow down the movement of the mouse, and this may be an appropriate strategy to use with some children.

## What should they be able to do?

At Year 1 level, children need to be aware of the ways in which information can be put into a computer. Talk to them about the wide range of uses IT has in the outside world, such as in supermarkets and banks, as well as making use of their own experiences of computers at home. Indeed, much of their initial work at school will be developing computer skills through the medium of games and other interactive activities.

During their time in Year 1, they should be taught how to put information into a computer using an ordinary keyboard, an overlay keyboard and a mouse. They should be able to put their name into a basic word-processor and subsequently write simple sentences, using a word bank and concept keyboard. They should also have experienced the use of a database for inputting information, understanding the use of the *cursor* and the *enter* key. They should be able to produce pictures using a paint program, making use of the *brush* tool. In all applications they should be able to print out work to a printer and to save their work to a floppy disk. Finally, they should be familiar with a simple floor robot, and be aware that it can be controlled remotely.

# Practical ideas

## Making a start

### Using talking story CD-ROMs

There is a wide range of these talking storybooks, many of which now originate in Great Britain and so have English voices and spellings. Each page usually consists of a brightly-coloured picture with some animation of the characters. A few sentences of text appear at a time, and each word is highlighted as it is spoken. Many contain a feature where clicking the mouse on particular parts of the picture makes further animations and sounds occur. You, or a helper, should sit with the children and listen to them repeat each sentence after it is spoken by the computer. Encourage the children to click on to particular graphic images to see the animations and hear the sounds that occur.

The computer skill (as opposed to reading skills) that is being developed here is control of the mouse, both in terms of movement and in using the mouse button to select particular words or actions on the screen. Make sure you keep a close eye on the way in which children's mouse skills develop. This is particularly important if you wish to avoid children gradually operating the mouse at arm's length, further and further away

from the computer itself. Encourage the children to pick the mouse up and reposition it on the mouse mat whenever this situation arises. Children who have acquired skill with the mouse can help other children to use it.

## Developing key areas

### Finding Teddy

This is a good introduction to a very important mouse skill called **click and drag** which is used extensively in all major computer programs.

Use a framework program such as *My World* that allows the children to fix already prepared images onto an existing background. (It can be best thought of as electronic fuzzy felt.) This is a program that can be used right through the primary age range, but the individual packages or screens are designed for specific age groups. One of the screens has Teddy hiding somewhere in a room. As you select each piece of furniture with a mouse click, it can then be moved to see if Teddy is behind it. A further mouse click will 'stick' it back to the background. If it is dragged over a picture of a dustbin, and then clicked, the selected object will disappear.

### Writing nursery rhymes

● Produce a concept keyboard overlay for a nursery rhyme. With some overlay editors it is possible to insert pictures into word processors as well as text. The content of the overlay can be as simple or complex as you wish. For example, it could include all the words of one nursery rhyme, but not in the correct order, together with one appropriate illustration. In this case the activity would be an ordering one, with the children recognising the words of the rhyme, putting them in the correct order, and then incorporating an illustration. You could ask the children to use the normal keyboard to type in their name at the bottom of the piece of work, before it is printed out and displayed. At this point, you should teach children to save their work onto floppy disks by using the *save*

command, and to print their work using a printer connected to their computer using the *print* command.

 Many variations of this activity are possible so that it can be adapted for children of different abilities. The children can be helped by having a copy of the nursery rhyme in front of them. You could include the words and pictures from two nursery rhymes, so that children have to be far more careful in their selection. Some of the easier words could be missed out of the overlay so that the children have to type these in themselves or, perhaps, if it is a very well-known rhyme, they could attempt to type in the words from memory. This activity is probably best done in pairs. In some cases, some peer tutoring might be appropriate, although the children who are acting as tutors must understand that they are helping and advising their partners – not doing it for them. Alternatively, children of similar skill level could work together, after being given strict guidance about sharing the actual time spent using the keyboard.

## Graph for eye and hair colour

Discuss with the class ways of collecting information on the colour of their eyes and hair. Working in pairs, one child collects the data about the other child, and they then enter the numbers into a database (the structure of which you have already prepared). This will require the children to locate the *cursor* in the correct column of the database and to press the *enter* key after typing in the data. When all the data has been collected, show the children the graph that is produced, explaining that it demonstrates the most common eye and hair colours. They can now discuss ways of collecting similar data from the whole year (or school), to see if the pattern is the same.

## Draw a picture of a meal

This could be part of a food topic. Using a paint package, children can draw a picture of a plate containing their favourite food and then type in their name. Provide them with a large circle for a plate as the starting point. Print out each meal as it is produced. When each child has completed the activity, use the pictures to create a game for the children to guess what each meal consists of. This activity will give practice in controlling the *brush* tool of the *paint* program using a mouse.

## Around the world

Give each child in the class the name of a foreign country and a picture of its flag. Using a word-processing program, they should type in the name of the country, making the text large. They should then find the flag in a clip-art collection and insert it underneath the name of the country. Print it out on a colour printer and display it on the wall. Alternatively, the children could colour in a black and white version. This activity will probably need to be done under close adult supervision, although some children in the class will master the technique quite quickly and will be able to help others.

## Ideas bank

### Bar chart of favourite toys

Up until now, most database activity has been based on whole-class work. Try asking small groups of children to input information about their favourite toys. You will probably still need to set up the structure of the database, although, by now, it can probably be done in discussion with the children.

### Carrying a message

Once children are familiar with the floor robot, set them the task of carrying a message from one area of the classroom to another by programming the robot.

### Draw a picture of your school

Children can use a paint package to draw a picture of their school. This will encourage them to use straight lines for the edges of buildings, windows and doors. This can be combined with geography work on maps and plans.

# Assessment

By the end of Year 1 you would expect most children to:

- use IT as part of their work in a number of curriculum areas;
- have used a number of story book CD-ROMs and be able to use a mouse to interact with the program;
- produce word-processed text using an overlay keyboard;
- write simple sentences using an ordinary keyboard;
- correct mistakes by using the *delete* key;
- print work out using the *print* command and save work on a disk using the *save* command;
- produce some artwork involving shapes and patterns using an art package, making use of the mouse to control the *brush* tool;
- input data into a simple database making use of the *cursor* and the *enter* key;
- present data graphically, and be able to talk about the graphs produced;
- control a simple floor robot, making it move forwards and backwards and to the left and right;
- make a robot perform a particular set of actions.

# Design and Technology

Designing and making should both be practised in Year 1 in a variety of contexts and with a range of materials. The aim is to develop children's design and technology capability, a combination of know-how and know-what. Some specific technological knowledge and understanding is to be developed but design and technology also draws on and consolidates learning in other areas. The contexts for design and technology activities will often be drawn from the themes and topics you are using. Examples of activities are described below. You may use them directly, adapt them or use them as models for other activities.

Some design and technology activities in Year 1 will develop awareness, knowledge and understanding. For instance, a toy might illustrate the wheel and axle mechanism, a pencil case could be used to show ways of joining fabrics, while a book might show how pages are gathered and bound. Such artefacts may be examined, mentally disassembled, have their parts named and their actions explained. Other objects may be physically dismantled, such as a box of tea-bags, with its several layers of wrapping, each with different properties.

Some activities used in Year 1 should develop particular designing or making skills. These focused practical tasks engage the children's attention through a context and lead to some product. Children may practise cutting thin plastics with snips, for instance, but the product they make is a plant label for the cress they are growing in science. By themselves, these tasks are unlikely to provide sufficient opportunity for the children to develop and show their designing and making capabilities, but they may be extended into a practical problem to solve which allows the child to try some independent designing and making. The likelihood of success is increased by limiting the materials and discussing some ways of using them.

wheel and axle
mechanism

It is important to incorporate opportunities for progression in design and technology capability. Over the year, the contexts should develop the children's awareness of materials into knowledge of their properties. They need to sense some properties directly by handling the materials. However, you will find it helps in designing and making if you provide materials in forms and sizes which relate to the task. The aim is to involve the children in some working of the material but this has to be manageable for those who lack manipulative skills and expertise in using tools. Nothing can be more de-motivating than a large box of thick cardboard with a pair of scissors quite inadequate for cutting it.

Various ways of joining and fastening are introduced and some quality of finish is encouraged, as in the production of an even cover of paint. Children with different capabilities

can often attempt the same task and, in essence, this is differentiation by outcome. You may tune a task to particular children's capabilities by the amount of support you provide and the reserve you show in intervening. The same problem may also be set with different degrees of openness: *We need to keep our tables tidy. What can we make to help us do that?* rather than *What can we make to stand our rulers and pencils in?* One can be easier than another.

Year 1 children should develop some skill in using simple hand tools although they may still lack some fine motor skills and act thoughtlessly. This means that safety will be a major consideration. Plan for safe working when deciding what activities to use. Remember to consider the safety of the child using the tool, and the safety of others, including yourself. Check tools regularly and withdraw from use any that could be unsafe. Repair or replace these as soon as possible. The area where the children are working with the tools should always be in view. Store tools securely when not in use. Encourage Year 1 children to be aware of dangers, to bring them to your attention and to avoid them.

# What should they be able to do?

When they begin Year 1, children will have made some things using materials like paper, card, fabrics, foodstuffs, kits and reclaimed materials. The form and size of these materials will have been well-suited to the task. They will have followed simple instructions to make their products and had the opportunity to extend some of the tasks as they thought appropriate. Their awareness of the made world will be growing and they will have dismantled and re-assembled a few simple items.

This experience is built on in Year 1 by developing children's awareness of the manufactured world; of what counts as important in design and technology capability; by providing opportunities to widen familiar contexts and extend them; by developing and extending designing and making skills; and by increasing their technological knowledge and understanding.

## Key area: Contexts

Design and technology activities drawn from your broader topics can help to integrate the curriculum but it may mean that some aspects of design and technology may be neglected. Deficiencies should be made good through a separate topic for design and technology on some occasions. In Year 1, such contexts and activities will tend to relate to the home, the school and the immediate environment so that the children will see their relevance.

## Key area: Making skills

By the end of Year 1 most children should:
- know which tools are appropriate for working some common materials;
- have developed manipulative skills in using tools for working some materials, such as paper, card, thin plastic sheet, strip wood, food and textiles;
- be able to give reasons for the choice of a particular material for a given task;
- use templates to replicate shapes and make simple templates;
- follow instructions;
- try to make practical suggestions about what to do next;
- be able to measure (by comparison) and mark out what they need;

- know how to join or combine some common materials and components;
- have extended and practised their finishing skills.

## Key area: Designing skills

Designing skills are needed for practical problem solving. The practical problems you provide should give children opportunities to suggest ideas for solving them. This often means that you will need to help the children recall experiences which contain a part of a solution. Help them synthesise the parts by discussion. If necessary, hint at possible solutions and provide potentially useful clues. Support them as they express and clarify their ideas and watch for those who incorporate effects which are only imaginary. (For instance, a child given the problem of making a simple toy may pretend that the wheels turn when, in fact, the model is supposed to have freely-turning wheels.) Encourage the children to practise ways of communicating their ideas. These may be through drawings and description, supplemented by a 'model' of the shape of the finished object using items that are to hand.

If you use PLAN-DO-REVIEW sheets in Year 1, you will find that they have a natural place in design and technology. Planning may be interpreted to cover designing, doing may be related to making, and reviewing can share features with evaluating.

By the end of the year most children should be able to communicate their ideas verbally and by simple drawings.

## Key area: Knowledge and understanding
### Materials and components

When more than one material might be used in a task (perhaps fabric and card), avoid introducing more than one new material at any one time, particularly if the children will need time to practise working with them. Sometimes it is better to supply only familiar materials so that working skills can be consolidated. While it may be possible to use a wide range of materials (possibly paper, card, plastics, wood or fabrics) they should be available in forms which can be readily manipulated by Year 1 children (such as 1cm square section wood strip and thin plastic sheet). Components at this stage include parts of kits and collections of card boxes and tubes.

By the end of the year, most children should be able to select materials appropriate to a task.

### Mechanisms and control

In Year 1, children need to learn the distinction between fixed joints and those which will allow movement. (They may make an animal which can turn its head but has fixed legs.) They should also extend their repertoire of ways of making joints (by using a stapler, for example). Energy to make things move will often be provided by the children themselves or by gravity.

*Design and technology*

## Structures

The children should develop an understanding of how the strength of a material depends on its size and thickness. In particular, they need to feel how a broad strip of thin material will bend more easily in one direction than the other. They should learn some ways to stiffen this type of shape (by thickening it, reinforcing it with a stronger material or by changing its shape).

## Products and applications

Children should investigate how simple products have been made, assembled and finished so that they suit their purpose. Toys, common classroom objects and safe household items are often suitable for this purpose. At this stage, they might compare several different versions of a product and evaluate them. Looking at stools or chairs, for example, they could identify features intended to make them comfortable (their shape or padding), safer to use (stability and a smooth finish), and features which reduce wear on other things (rubber feet).

## Quality

Children should be encouraged to have some concern for the quality of the product in terms of how well it is made (perhaps how well the parts will be able to carry the expected load).

## Health and safety

Develop in the children an interest in avoiding injury to themselves and others. Most Year 1 children should be able to demonstrate the safe use of the tools they use and they should show some awareness of potential hazards and a willingness to avoid them.

## Vocabulary

During the year, the children's vocabulary for what they use and do will be extended through the needs of the particular contexts they encounter (*wrapper, smooth finish, even spread*).

# Working at higher or lower levels within the key areas

Sometimes, working at other levels is achieved by altering the degree of support you provide. While it is always possible to provide simpler tasks with different contexts, this can make a child's inadequacies, real or otherwise, visible to all. One good alternative you might try is to use a context which allows a variety of possible products (such as a playground). You might then allocate tasks according to each child's ability, thus ensuring that everyone is working at an appropriate level.

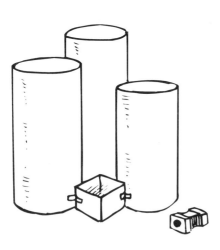

Children with well-developed design and technology capabilities can be stretched by providing extension tasks which develop their product beyond the original brief. A desk tidy, for instance, might have a compartment added for a pencil sharpener.

# Practical ideas

## Making a start

You may be working on a broad topic such as Clothes or you may be focused on a particular area of the curriculum such as Science (Things which Float). These can generate design and technology work on, for instance, fabrics (exploration of their variety and nature), or on water transport (boats). The children's interest may be caught by an artefact, a picture, a story or a visit which sets the scene for a problem. The children should be taught to clarify their design ideas by responding to *What? Why? How?* questions and by describing and justifying their intentions. While making, they should be aware of what is, and what is not, going well. *What could you do next?*

### Providing contexts

Children need to see purpose and interest in what they do. You will also have to encourage them to relate prior knowledge and know-how to the task in hand. Some of the following strategies may prove useful.

### Visits

Visits do not have to be prolonged or distant to be useful. For instance, a visit to a playground can be used to develop children's descriptive vocabulary of the structures (*pole, hollow tube, criss-cross tubing, chute*) and could then lead to designing and making a model playground for the classroom. (See page 148.)

### Stories

Stories which relate to the properties of the materials used are particularly useful, so a story about Hansel and Gretel and the wicked witch's edible house could be used to introduce biscuit or gingerbread making. (See page 149.)

### Visitors

Parents often have hobbies which can have a useful place in the design and technology classroom - someone keen on DIY may be willing to make a bird table in the classroom. This could then be used in other areas of the curriculum, such as Science.

## Supporting making
### Materials, skills and quality

Much support for making comes from what you do before the lesson. Materials that are limited in range point the children in the right direction. So if they are making a comb-case (see page 148) you can limit the quantity, type and shape of the fabric. Using felt rather than a fabric which frays simplifies the task. During any activity, your demonstration of how to make something should be an example of good practice. Talk about what you are doing as you demonstrate or guide children through a task. Have clear targets of what will count as quality in a particular task (symmetry, an even coat of paint, straight cuts). Show your own concern for quality and praise it in the children's products.

### Designing and problem solving
### Exploring the task

You will need to ensure that the children know what the task means and what it encompasses. Ask questions to stimulate the recall of relevant prior knowledge and practise new vocabulary. Supplement knowledge so that the task is meaningful. Ask for ideas and be prepared to provide hints and clues. Put items (like boxes and tubes) together loosely and use them to give concrete, visible form to the children's ideas (*Is this what you mean? No? You show me.*) This demonstrates a way of communicating ideas that you need to encourage in the children.

### Developing new knowledge

Artefacts can be useful for developing new knowledge, particularly if they are everyday objects and safe to handle. Let the children examine them and explain how they work.

 ## Introducing new ideas

### Designing and making

In each of the examples below (a) is the introduction, (b) is a related practical task, and (c) develops it further. They may be used as they are, they may be adapted, or they could serve as models for other activities.

#### Components: card box animals

(a) Within topics such as Dinosaurs or Pets, examine pictures and identify the common features of animals (head, neck, body, legs, tail).

(b) Using large and small boxes for head and body and card tubes for neck and legs, assemble an animal. Show how, by pushing a tube into a star-shaped hole (see illustration), a 'free joint' can be made so that the head can turn on the tube neck. The legs should be fixed in place with adhesive (fixed joint). The animal may now be completed by painting it or by covering it with stuck-on fabrics. Add a tail, ears and a tongue.

(c) The children now design and make animals of their choice. The models can be assembled as a 'herd' in a corner of the classroom against an appropriate background.

#### Fabrics: comb case

(a) One starting point could be to make a gift for a special occasion. Another might be in Health Education (personal hygiene and care over appearance).
(b) Show the children how to make a template in card by drawing around a comb, leaving a large margin for joining. Show them how to use the template to cut out two matching pieces of felt. Staple the pieces together, leaving one end open for the comb.

(c) The children make a comb case as above and may then stick on coloured pieces of felt to make a pattern or figure. A variant is for them to try sewing the felt with running stitches instead of using staples. An extension would be to make a pencil case or purse in the same way. This presents the additional problem of designing a fastener for the case or purse.

### Recycled materials: adventure playground

(a) Visit a local playground to explore the structures and the kinds of activity available, or look at pictures of playgrounds.

(b) Discuss with the children what they would like in an adventure playground. Explore with them how they might model these items from reclaimed materials. Roughly assemble one or two from the available materials to make the ideas concrete, if necessary.

(c) Working in small groups, the children make an item for a class adventure playground. Display these as a group on a surface which simulates grass and against an appropriate frieze. As an extension, the children could design and make seats, litter bins and shrubs for the scene.

### Wood: a helping hand

(a) Make a collection of pliers, pincers, tweezers, salad tongs and so on to introduce the tools which help us pick things up and hold them. Make a

very large pair of pliers from card and a paper fastener. Let the children try them and compare them with the artefacts. Help them identify weaknesses in this model (*the soft card tends to be rather floppy and does not grip well*) and perhaps consider methods of improvement.

(b) Ask: *Who do you think might need a 'picker-upper'?* Explore this need by asking *When?* and *Why?* questions. Point out the weaknesses of the card model. *What else could we use?* If necessary, show them lengths of strip wood (1cm square section, approximately). Encourage the children to think through how they will make a picker-upper from the strip wood. *Instead of a pivot, what might you use?* (perhaps a rubber band holding the centres of the strips together, like pliers, or a card hinge stuck to the ends of the strips, like salad tongs).

(c) The children now test their picker-uppers to evaluate their effectiveness in general, and then on small and round objects. The need for further development will be apparent. *How can the ends of the tongs be made to grip objects better?* Help the children with their ideas (they may suggest attaching sandpaper or pieces of felt to the ends) and let them try them out.

## Food: a house to eat

(a) Begin by reading a version of the Hansel and Gretel story.

(b) Make a biscuit mix and have the children spoon the mixture onto a non-stick tray to make a large biscuit for each of them. Bake the biscuits (including a few spares). While they are cooling, show the children how to pipe ready-made fondant icing to make a picture.

(c) The children now draw their proposed house shape on paper. If you can supply other cake decorations and a selection of food colours for the icing they could include these in their designs. They then copy the designs onto the biscuits using the icing and decorations.

## ❀ Ideas bank

### Desk tidy

When the children have become disorganised with their pencils, crayons and so on, point out how useful it would be to have something to keep these tidy on their tables. Holders can be made from reclaimed materials. Long, narrow boxes may be joined to vertical tubes to serve as pencil and ruler holders.

## Special things box

Ask the children to examine a large box (a cereal box, for example) to see how it is made. Help them open its seams and show how it can be turned inside out and re-glued so that clean, clear surfaces are now on the outside. They could try this in making a box to keep special things in. This may be painted and have pictures stuck on according to the child's tastes and interests. Turning boxes inside out to present clean surfaces in this way can be useful know-how.

## Notice boards

Draw the children's attention to notices, notice boards and their purpose. Have them examine one to see how it is made, drawing attention to the soft board into which pins can be stuck. The children can make simple notice boards from the sides of card boxes. These can be cut to any shape the children choose (perhaps animals or fruit) and can have fabric stuck to them. If fabric is used, the boards tend to bend as they dry so it is a good idea to leave them under a flat, heavy surface for a while. If the children also make weather symbols, these boards may serve as

'Today's Weather' boards.

## Labelling things

Plastic boxes (which have held ice-cream, margarine and so on) provide a source of free, thin plastic sheet. Children can use this material to design and make waterproof labels (for plant pots or garden frames). The plastic can be cut into various shapes and can be written on with permanent marker pens or over-head projector pens.

## Carrying things

Engineer an event in which your carrier bag bursts and spills its contents of bulky, light boxes on the classroom floor. Draw the children's attention to the need for an effective carrier bag. Challenge them to make one from the limited materials you have provided (a large sheet of newsprint paper or sugar paper, a limited amount of adhesive tape and a few paper clips). You will probably need to discuss the handle design. On completion, bags can be finished with a logo or other motif. The bags may then be tested with the bulky, light objects.

## A farmyard

After a visit to a farm or having watched a television programme about a farm, the children could design and make a farmyard from reclaimed materials, each group contributing a separate item. These could be displayed collectively against an appropriate background. Lollipop sticks can be used to make fences and gates.

## Figures with articulating joints

To widen children's experience of freely-turning joints, a study of doll figure articulation (for example Action People) and of an art mannequin can be useful. Make sure the purpose of the task is clear and ask questions which focus upon how the movement is achieved. They can make a figure of themselves from card, using paper fasteners to make moveable joints at the shoulders, elbows, hips and knees. These can be displayed hanging in a row along a wall.

## Make a book

An old book which is about to be thrown out may be carefully dismantled to see how its pages are bound together. This activity could precede the children putting together a book of their own work.

## Picture frames

To extend experience in using strip wood, children can make picture frames by gluing strips of wood together, strengthening the corners with small triangles of card. This activity becomes more challenging if the children start with a small picture which the frame must fit.

## Transparent toys for study

Disassembly does not always mean that the children physically dismantle a product. It can mean that they study it and figure out what its components do. Some toys have transparent bodies for this purpose. The ways in which they are constructed are visible and coloured moving parts can be observed in action. You need to make the task purposeful by asking specific questions, such as: *Can you see how the top is fastened on? What are those things called? What happens to the red part when the car goes?*

# Assessment

In Design and Technology, both knowledge and skills are to be assessed. While a product can provide some evidence of skills, it cannot tell you everything. In particular, you need to know about those skills which do not show themselves in a product. Did the children suggest ideas? Did they suggest what to do next? Did they work tidily and carefully? Did they use equipment appropriately? To assess these things you need to observe them as they work.

## What do they know?

They should:

- know some properties of materials like paper, card, thin plastics, fabrics, foodstuffs and wood;
- have vocabulary which helps them describe these properties, such as hard, soft, bendy, stiff, rough, smooth, waterproof, see-through;
- know ways of modifying some of these properties (smoothing with sandpaper, stiffening by increasing the thickness or number of layers);
- know which cutting/shaping tools and techniques, such as means of fixing, are appropriate for the materials in the tasks.

## What can they do?

They should:

- begin to use their technological experiences to generate simple ideas;
- begin to communicate their ideas with pictures, words, and simple, loosely-arranged models, using materials to hand;
- use tools safely;
- be able to assemble and join some materials in more than one way;
- be able to describe their products and say what purpose they serve;
- be able to provide some simple evaluation of their products in terms of suitability for their task. Occasionally, they should be able to suggest an improvement;
- be able to describe a simple, familiar object and how it works (possibly hand tools like pliers).

# Religious Education

Religious education, unlike other subjects of the National Curriculum, has to be planned from a local rather than a national document. Agreed Syllabuses differ in the way they present the programme of study but are remarkably similar in what they expect children to do in RE. It is very likely that your Agreed Syllabus expects children to:

- develop a knowledge and understanding of religious traditions;
- explore fundamental questions arising out of people's experience of life;
- develop their own ideas and values arising partly out of what they learn in RE.

In terms of continuity and progression in RE, you should be helping the children to develop a systematic knowledge and understanding of some religions, as well as developing their thinking about religious issues, and grasp of common themes across religions which will contribute to their understanding of religion in general.

RE can be approached through 'human experience' topics which focus on an important issue or question about life such as *Who is my neighbour?* or *How should we care for our world?* This second question is used as the basis for the topic presented in this chapter (see page 155) where children are encouraged to consider some fundamental questions about the natural world. These questions and issues are then explored by looking at a number of religious responses to them. This example can serve as a model for handling other themes with this age group.

Children in their early years do not learn about religious traditions in a systematic way. The concept of a tradition like Christianity or Judaism will mean very little to them. Later in the primary school they will need to be introduced to such ideas but, for the first two years at least, they will learn about aspects of religions within the context of their own experience and broader general themes. This approach lends itself to exploring religious education through integrated themes or topics. This is entirely appropriate as long as there is coherence across the curriculum. The topic in this chapter, 'Caring for our World', can be linked to science (Life Processes and Living Things) or geography (a thematic study on the quality of the environment). However in RE topics your emphasis should be on:

- helping the children to develop certain significant concepts derived from both human experience and religious traditions;

● raising questions that are essentially spiritual in nature and being aware of the children's responses to these.

# What should they be able to do?

Year 1 children will be aware of some relevant features of the natural world such as changes in the weather, the seasons and, in some cases, that natural things can die or decay. Many children of this age, as they become aware that the world exists outside themselves, begin to ask quite profound questions about the meaning of things, such as: *Who made the world?* or, on the death of a pet: *What will happen to him now?* It is important that you encourage them to develop their language by helping them formulate such questions about the world around them. Their ability to respond will vary, but most children at this age should be able to listen to appropriate stories and talk about their experiences of the natural world. Many will be able to engage in discussions and offer an opinion, although at this stage you should not be too concerned about different levels of response. In Year 1 the very fact that they respond at all is what you should be looking for. Bearing this in mind, the following is a guide to what most Year 1 children should be expected to do and understand in relation to three key areas of RE.

## Key area: Knowledge and understanding of religions

Children at this age develop their knowledge and understanding through direct contact with people, concrete situations and stories. They do not, in general, develop their knowledge and understanding of religions in a systematic way. This theme provides a structure for exploring some key ideas from religious traditions about the relationship between human beings and the natural world.

The aspects of religious responses to the natural world that are explored in this topic are questions about creation and human responsibility for it, and about our dependency on the Earth's resources.

### Concept development

Concept development is an essential component of good RE teaching at any level. The range of religious concepts that can be explored in this topic include **creation, stewardship** and **ahimsa** (pronounced ah-him-sa, an Indian religious concept which means 'harmlessness' or 'reverence for all living things'). The children should be introduced to such technical vocabulary and be allowed to understand it at their own level. For example, most Year 1 children will understand ahimsa as meaning 'being kind to other creatures'.

The best way of introducing children to such concepts is through story, and particular examples from religions, shown in pictures or on video. This is the method followed in the practical ideas section of this chapter (page 156).

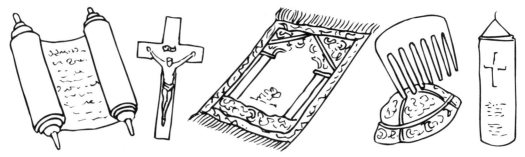

# Raising fundamental questions

Another vital aspect of good RE teaching is the raising of fundamental questions, although this does not mean that the children shouldn't learn facts about particular religions. They do need to gain some knowledge of Christian and Jewish Harvest festivals, for example, but much of the knowledge and understanding that they have to grasp about religious traditions is set within the context of questions like: *How does God think we should treat the Earth? Does God want us to be kind to animals? Why do people celebrate Harvest?* (There are other relevant questions that can be explored in this topic. These are dealt with under the other two key areas.)

## Key area : Exploring human experience

This topic provides opportunities for the children to explore and reflect on the wonders of nature and to hear stories about human responsibility for the Earth and its creatures.

Your aim in this area is to develop the children's awareness of the world around them. Much of their work in science and geography on life processes and the environment will help to do this. In RE, however, the focus should be on specific concepts and types of question.

Concepts that you can encourage them to discuss include: responsibility, wonder, mystery, care, pattern, beauty, change.

From discussions about such ideas you can help them explore questions such as: *How should we treat the Earth?* These questions are not only important in themselves but they form a base from which the children can approach the stories and experiences relating to the first key area.

## Key area: Responding to religion and human experience

Responding to questions plays an essential role in this element. Encourage the children to respond individually to the type of questions outlined in the other key areas. Show them how to answer such questions with statements that begin with 'I think...' or 'I believe...'. This will help them to appreciate that people can respond to important questions in their own way, which, in turn, will encourage them to develop respect for another person's point of view. If you give children this opportunity, some of them may be able to begin to make connections between their own feelings and how others have responded to the natural world. It should also encourage them to learn to respect and care for the world. Such positive attitudes are essential if the children are to understand the concepts explored in the other key areas.

Most children should be able to express their responses to what they have learned through various media such as drawing pictures, making up prayers or writing simple stories.

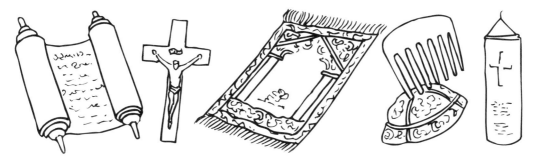

# Practical ideas

Religious education

## ❀ Making a start

### Go on a walk

Arrange to take the class on a nature walk. You could do this on a single day with the class split into groups, or take a different group out on a number of occasions. Concentrate on encouraging the children to look for things, to listen and to smell. Prepare them by talking about, and showing them, examples of patterns in natural things, such as the rings of a tree or fungi (especially in the autumn). On your return, ask them to respond through a variety of forms such as art, music, writing, discussion and silence. If you want children to use silence effectively you will have to guide them in this.

### Use guided fantasy

● A good way to encourage reflection is the technique of guided fantasy which makes use of music and/or words. You begin by asking the children to relax and to develop a still mind. If you can meditate, teach them how this is done. Then select a subject, perhaps a leaf, and get them to imagine that they are leaves falling from a tree. Play some soothing music.

● An excellent source of ideas for quiet, reflective, spiritual activities is *Don't Just Do Something; Sit There* by Mary K Stone (Religious and Moral Education Press). This book is a very useful resource because it provides practical exercises which help children to learn how to be still and to use reflection effectively. There is a chapter on creative visualisation which fits in with this topic. Particularly useful is the work on leaves, stones and creating a special place in nature.

### Show a video or a picture

Try to get hold of either a large format picture of the Earth in space (for example, Westhill Project, Life Themes in the Early Years Pack 1) or a video such as Michael Jackson's recording of 'Earthsong'. You could use both. After showing them the picture and/or playing the video, ask the children some appropriate questions so that you can begin a conversation about caring for the Earth. *What do you see in this picture? What is Michael Jackson singing about? Who lives on the Earth? Is the Earth the only planet? Has it always been here? How did it begin? Will it always be here? What kinds of things do people, plants and animals need to live on our planet? In what ways could our planet be made a better place for people to live?*

### Read a story

Read the children a story that raises questions about how we should treat the Earth. An excellent book for this is Michael Foreman's *Dinosaurs and All That Rubbish* (Penguin). Alternatively choose his more recent book *One World*.

Discuss with the class some of the issues and meanings that arise from the story. Use some prompt questions such as: *What do you think about the way the man treated the Earth? How should we treat the Earth? Is the Earth precious? Why? Who does the Earth belong to? Should we share the Earth with animals? What can we do to care for the Earth?*

### Sing a song

There are plenty of hymns and songs in the *Come and Praise* series (BBC Books) like 'Think of a World Without Any Colours', 'From a Tiny Ant' or 'All the Animals' which are suitable for this theme.

### Pictures, poems and prayers

Ask the children to draw pictures and write poems and prayers about the world to tell other people of its beauties. Compile these into a class book.

## ❀ Introducing new key areas

You can extend the topic by focusing specifically on the relationship between humans and animals. The following activities introduce the children to various ways in which animals are regarded and to specific stories and knowledge which can increase their capacity to reflect on appropriate questions. Always try to keep the questioning open and try not to act as the only reference point for answers. The type of questions that enable

children to respond most fully are those suggested in the following activities.

## Show some pictures

Show the children pictures of an assortment of animals - some wild, some tame, some ugly, some pretty. Ask them questions like: *Why do we like some animals and not others? Are animals as important as people? Should we kill or eat animals? Do animals feel like we do? Should we kill ants and flies? What about wasps?*

## Tell a story

There are a number of stories from the religious traditions which are suitable for exploring some of the questions listed above. One of the best is 'Mohammed and the Ants' from a book called *Love All God's Creatures* published by The Islamic Foundation. Alternatively you could read or tell stories of St. Francis. Discuss some of the issues and meanings in the stories.

## Discuss a picture

● Try to obtain a picture of a Jain monk from a resource centre. Jainism emphasises the idea of ahimsa (reverence for all living things). A monk will wear a gauze mask so as not to breathe in anything and uses a brush to sweep the ground free of tiny creatures so as not to step on them.

Talk about this with the children. *Is it practical for all of us? Can you think of any ways in which we could be kinder to animals?* Children can draw a picture of the monk and write a few sentences explaining the picture.

● Alternatively show them a picture of Krishna and cows. These brightly-coloured Hindu bazaar pictures are readily available in resource centres and from a number of suppliers (see list on page 159). Explain that the cow is sacred for Hindus. All cows are treated very specially in India and nobody is allowed to harm one because they represent Mother Earth. You should explore with the children what the word 'sacred' means. (Focus on things that are very special. A church is a very special place, a cow is a very special animal for Hindus.) On a more mundane level, ask the children to think of all the ways in which a cow is useful to people in India. Remember that, because the cow is sacred, Hindus will not eat beef.

## Make up a story

Ask the children to make up a simple story called 'A day in the life of an animal'. Allow them to choose which animal. Help them by discussing some of the things they have learned about and discussed in previous lessons.

## Invite a visitor

A number of local authorities have an 'Animal Man' who comes into school to show children various creatures. Invite him in for an assembly or to your class.

## ✿ Developing key areas

## Knowledge and understanding of religions

### Learn about harvest

● A good way of extending children's learning in this key area is to introduce them to how and why some religious groups celebrate harvest. You could choose the Christian celebration and one other. Jewish Sukkot is a good one but, if you work in a school with a large number of Hindu children, you may prefer to investigate Holi from the Hindu tradition. Try always to link the

information about the religions to questions of human experience. Present the festivals as ways that people understand and respond, in a religious way, to some of the questions you have been discussing in this topic. Some children may be able to talk about their own experience of the festivals.

● Ask your resource centre for pictures of Harvest festivals and Sukkot or Holi. These will probably come with information which will help you to inform the children about these festivals. Talk about where our food comes from and encourage them to think of as many ways as possible in which we harvest the fruits of the earth. Make a collection of pictures showing combine harvesters and tractors at work, fruit pickers, trawler men and so on.

### Build a 'sukkah'

Collect a lot of branches and greenery and use them to build your own small hut, or 'sukkah', in a corner of the classroom. Have a celebratory meal of unleavened bread and a wine substitute (perhaps grape or blackcurrant juice) to mark its completion. Explain to the children that Jewish families often eat meals together in a Sukkah during the eight days of the festival. (If you have any Jewish children in the class, encourage them to talk about what their families do at Sukkot.)

When you have talked about harvest and the festivals, most children will be able to write an account of how, and why, Christians and Jews or Hindus celebrate harvest. Other children can work with you, or a helper, on shared writing where you write down what they want to say.

### Assembly ideas

If the school is having a Harvest festival, your class will, of course, be involved and can paint pictures to decorate the hall, prepare some readings, bake bread, bring food from home and so on. But there are a number of other assembly themes which can arise from this topic. A good theme is **Beginnings**. You can construct an assembly around the song 'Morning Has Broken'. Talk about the words and ask questions like: *Can you imagine what the first morning was like? Do you think it was quiet or noisy? Sunny or frosty? What do you think made the first noise? Was it the blackbird?*

Show the children some man-made and natural objects and talk about how things are made. Explain that many people believe that natural things are made by God and that God created the world. Talk about the word 'create' and how it means to make something new. Many people also believe that, as in the song, God creates each new day so that we can create things for ourselves. Ask them what they can create for themselves (start some new work, paint a picture, write a poem, make a new friend and so on).

Develop your assembly from these discussions and the children's ideas.

## Creation stories

● Introduce a simple version of the Genesis creation story and read it to the children (one can be found in *Action plans: Assemblies* published by Scholastic, but there are many other versions, or you can tell the story yourself.) There is a rich variety of creation stories from many other cultures - you can find some of these in *A Tapestry of Tales* by Liz Breuilly and Sandra Palmer (Collins).

Encourage the children to paint the moment of creation. They should follow any ideas they have themselves, or use black sugar paper, red, yellow and white paint and a spatter technique to paint the first moment of creation.

## Books to read

A good source for prayers and readings is *Prayers for a Fragile World* by Carol Wilson (Lion).

There is a large collection of stories available that can stimulate children's reflections on all aspects of the natural world.

You'll find a comprehensive list in Maurice Lynch's book *Tell Me a Story* (available from the BFSS National RE Centre).

Here is a brief list of some particularly appealing books:
*A Tree is Nice* by Janice May Udry (World's Work).
*One Hungry Spider* by Jeannie Baker (André Deutsch).
*The Very Hungry Caterpillar* by Eric Carle (Picture Puffin).
*Where Are You Going, Emma?* by Jeanne Titherington (Julia Macrae).
*The People Who Hugged Trees* by Deborah Lee Rose (Roberts Reinhart).
*The Best of Children's Poetry* by J Curry (Red Fox).

## Resources and suppliers

Articles of Faith, 0161 763 6232
BFSS National RE Centre, Brunel University at the Osterley Campus, 0181 891 8324
National Society's RE Centre, 0171 932 1190
Westhill RE Centre, Birmingham, 0121 415 2258
Welsh National RE Centre, 01248 382952.

# Assessment

When you have finished this topic, you will have a good idea whether the children have enjoyed it. You should be able to judge by the outcomes how much they have learned, but evaluation can also take the following form.

## What do they know?

The emphasis in this topic is not, essentially, on knowledge of religions. However, from the experiences gained during the topic most children should know:

- some stories, including those from religious traditions, about caring for the world;
- a story about creation from a religion;
- some of the ways in which humans can care for the planet;
- some of the ways in which people show care for the Earth and its resources.

## What can they do?

In a typical Year 1 class you can expect children to respond at different levels. In this topic, for example, all, or most, of the children will be able to:

- talk about ways that they can care for the world;
- retell the basic elements of a story;
- express their ideas in written or visual forms.
  Some children will:
- understand and explain why humans need to care for the world;
- begin to be aware that humans are dependent on the Earth's resources;
- understand and explain why people who follow a religion behave in certain ways;
- explain something of the meaning of a story.

## What have they experienced?

The children should have:

- listened to stories about caring for the world;
- contributed to discussions;
- expressed their ideas in written and visual forms;
- learned about religious responses to the natural world through pictures and videos.

## How have they made their knowledge public?

Most children should have made a public display of their knowledge in writing and pictures and by contributing to discussions.